Uncommon Words
Often Used in
Print Journalism

Uncommon Words
Often Used in
Print Journalism

Jorge Lema-Patiño

VANTAGE PRESS
New York

AUTHOR'S NOTE

The objective of this book is to serve as a quick reference tool. This edition is addressed to students and professionals dedicated to current issues dealing with economic, social and political affairs. The "Uncommon Words Often Used in Print Journalism" are, as the title clearly states, used in the print media; this includes newspapers and magazines (*Time, Newsweek, The Washington Post,* etc.).

The book shall draw up the interest of foreigners and English-speaking people who, although they are proficient in the use of the English language, wish to acquire a better command of the written grammar and vocabulary.

Uncommon Words Often Used in Print Journalism

CHAPTER I

A–B WORDS

abet—v.   assist; encourage; aid; support
abetment—n.
abettor—n.   e: The woman who handed the killer the knife was charged with aiding and *abetting* the crime.
The driver of the getaway car was found guilty of *abetment.*
"aiding and abetting"

abeyance—n.   expectation; suspension; delay
e: Until the issue is clarified, it remains in *abeyance.*
The tenants held their rent in *abeyance* until repairs were made.
"hold in abeyance"—withhold something until another complies with a demand

abound—adj.   fully supplied; present in large number or quantity; plentiful
abundance—n.
abundant—adj.   e: Stress-management plans *abound*, but not all run well.
In the northern forests wild animals *abound.*

accrue—v.   increase; gain
accrual—n.
accruement—n.   e: The benefits of this weight-loss program *accrue* only to believers.
She left her money in the bank where it could *accrue* interest.

acquit—v.   clear of a charge or obligation; exonerate; pardon
acquittal—n.   e: The journalists were relieved that the judge *acquitted* them of *libeling* three policemen in a story on alleged brutality.
The defendant was *acquitted* due to insufficient evidence.
opposite: indict; convict

adamant—adj.   unshakable; immovable, determined, rigid
e: The rebuilding project is doomed because the tenants are *adamant* about not moving.
She is *adamant* in her refusal to participate, so we will have to find someone else.

1

adjourn—v.   suspend; move to another time; recess
adjournment—n.   e: The hearing was *adjourned* until next week. The meeting will commence promptly at noon and be *adjourned* at approximately 2:00 P.M.

admonish—v.   reprove; warn; advise
admonishment—n.
admonition—n.
admonitory—adj.   e: Publishers have been *admonished* to watch the political soundness of their work.
He was constantly *admonishing* his employees to stop wasting so much time.

adroit—adj.   skillful; clever
adroitness—n.   e: Reagan's political *adroitness* has helped him out of many difficult situations.
The lawyer was *adroit* at winning seemingly hopeless cases.

advocate—v.   support; plead for the cause of another; defender
advocate—n.
advocacy—n.   e: Consumer *advocates* warned the public of the company's poor reputation.
Conservatives on Capitol Hill are *advocating* further defense increases.
There is a conservative concern over socialist *advocacy* of more control of public education.

aegis—n.   protection; sponsorship; shield
e: The oil is under the *aegis* of Arab control.
The people are enjoying more freedom and prosperity under the *aegis* of the new constitution.
"Under the aegis of"—with the protection of

aftermath—n.   consequence; result
e: War and its *aftermath* have destroyed many formerly prospering industrial groups.
In the *aftermath* of recent Israeli elections of reactionaries, the Camp David accords seem tenuous.

ajar—adj.   partially open
e: The agreement left the door *ajar* to further changes in the law.
The new constitution left the door *ajar* to cooperation if opposition parties emerged.
"leave the door ajar to"—allow for a later action

alien—n.   person of another nation or race
alien—adj.
alienation—n.
alienate—v.   e: The number of illegal *aliens* arrested along the U.S.–Mexican border jumped dramatically.
Most *aliens* are forbidden to seek employment during their travels to our country.

allure—n.   power to entice; fascination; to seduce or tempt
lure—v.   e: They raised millions in the last few years before the senate elections, even without the *allure* of a presidential race.
Wearing such an *alluring* dress is not suitable to your respected position.

alter—v.   change; transform; modify

alteration—n.   e: Participants voted unanimously to *alter* bylaws to allow more outside participation.

Because her earlier tactics had failed, she *altered* her approach.

amass—v.   collect; accumulate

amassment—n.   e: The recent discovery in Chile is the largest stash of weapons ever *amassed* in Latin America.

Over many years of diplomatic service, the ambassador has *amassed* an impressive private book collection.

amiable—adj.   pleasant; friendly; congenial

amiability—n.

amiableness—n.   e: She is usually very helpful; I expect that she will be *amiable* to our suggestions.

The upturning profits put the director in an *amiable* frame of mind.

amiss—adj.   out of proper order; wrong

e: Some people see nothing *amiss* in the growing gap between the rich and the poor.

I have been *amiss* in the way I've treated you; I'll try to show more respect.

appall—v.   fill with horror, dismay, or disgust; shock

e: We were *appalled* by the news of the beloved mayor's corruption.

His *appalling* behavior at the reception embarrassed me deeply.

apt—adj.   well fitted or qualified; clever; appropriate

e: The wine was *aptly* chosen; that was a good year in the Rhine Valley.

"Criminal" is an *apt* label for her horrible behavior.

arraign—v.   call before court; accuse; indict

arraignment—n.   e: Epstein was *arraigned* yesterday on charges of grand larceny.

He is presently being held by police; the *arraignment* will take place tomorrow.

array—n.   impressive group or arrangement (often military); display

array—v.   e: He was urging quick steps to reduce the *array* of risks facing the economy.

The bank offers an *array* of savings options from which to choose.

asking price—n.   price at which something is offered for sale   e: Argentina's *asking price* for propping up U.S. initiatives and plans was considered to be too high.

The *asking price* for most commodities has been falling lately.

assail—v.   attack (verbally); leap upon

assailant—n.   e: They *assailed* the castle walls, hoping to steal the treasure inside.

The West German industry *assailed* the Bonn government for its fiscal policies.

The *assailants* beat the old man and then ran away with his money.

assert—v.   declare; defend; affirm; aggressive

assertion—n.

assertive—adj.   e: Mr. Nakasone governs with a more *assertive* style than is normally found in Japan.

The police moved in to *assert* central governmental authority in West Beirut.

He is a very *assertive* individual.

assuage—v.   satisfy; ease; relieve; alleviate
   e: In the president's address he sought to *assuage* the doubts of his leadership abilities.
   His calm manner helped to *assuage* her fears.

avert—v.   turn away; avoid
aversion—n.
aversive—adj.
averse—adj.   e: It is important to *avert* any upsurge in inflation.
   The strike was *averted* by a last-minute compromise.

avid—adj.   enthusiastic; vigorous
   e: He was an *avid* baseball fan; he was at the park every weekend.
   When he returns to California, Reagan is an *avid* horseback rider.

awe—v.   inspire dread or fear; amaze
awe—n.
awesome—adj.   e: He was *awed* by her presence and could not speak to her.
   God is viewed with *awe* by many.

awry—adj.   turned or twisted position; amiss
   e: Something was *awry* at the office; everyone was acting unnatural.
   All his plans had gone *awry* because of the drop in oil prices.

back away—v.   move back; withdraw
   e: To seek accord the governor *backed away* from his controversial education cuts.
   She *backed away* from the deal because he refused to furnish important details.

backbite—v.   speak spitefully of someone not present; defame
   e: *Backbiting* among members in the movement caused it to become ineffective.
   We cannot tolerate such *backbiting*; please confine your remarks to the facts.

backlash—n.   sudden backward movement; strong adverse reaction
   e: A call for peace talks from El Salvador's leftist rebels has provoked an angry *backlash*
   from this country's right wing.
   The student protests have created a *backlash* against their supporters in the government.

bail out—v.   1. provide money to release an accused person from jail;
   2. rescue, aid;
   3. parachute from a plane
bail—n.   e: She *bailed* him *out* so that he wouldn't have to spend the night in jail.
   The government has refused to *bail out* bankrupt private companies simply to preserve
   jobs.
   The pilot *bailed out* of his plane when it was hit.

balk—v.   stop abruptly; foil; refuse
   e: He *balked* over future talks on nuclear disarmament, saying that the situation was
   not yet appropriate.
   His plan to take over the corporation was *balked* by an arrangement among the
   managers.

4

batter—v.   bombard; beat heavily; damage repeatedly
e: The attacking army appears to have been *battered* and bloodied by its costly victory.
Inflationary times have left many *battered* corporations trying desperately to survive.

bearish—adj.   expecting a fall in stock market prices; pessimistic; conquer; defeat
bear—n.   e: *Bearish* factors are appearing every day in the newspapers; sell now!
The short-term outlook for most commodities is decidedly *bearish* because the recession shows no sign of turning around.

bear out—v.   substantiate; confirm
e: The president's predictions that the recession would end in 1982 were not *borne out* by events—it continued well into 1983.
Experience has *borne out* the fact that inflation must be carefully controlled or it can ruin a country.

bedlam—n.   place or scene of confusion or chaos; anarchy; commotion
e: The tanks moved up to the marines' tanks amidst a *bedlam* of wild gunfire.
The outrageous proposal turned the meeting hall into a scene of *bedlam.*

bedraggle—v.   to make exhausted, wet, limp, or soiled, to soak
e: The *bedraggled* refugees have been fleeing for years.
Since the recession began, more and more *bedraggled* people have shown up at the city shelters every day.

beef up—v.   reinforce; build up
e: We need to *beef up* the competence of our teachers or they will produce a generation of illiterates.
Although many people are calling for arms reductions, some would like to see NATO's nuclear force *beefed up* some more.

befuddle—v.   confuse; perplex
befuddlement—n.   e: The unpredictable turns in the economy have *befuddled* the administration; they cannot seem to give a convincing explanation.
Some customers complain that they are *befuddled* by the numerous new banking options.

beguile—v.   deceive; divert
e: How did he manage to *beguile* you into buying damaged goods?
The president was *beguiled* by the neighboring leaders' friendliness and was not prepared when they attacked.

belated—adj.   delayed; appearing past the normal time; slow; tardy
e: I forgot that her birthday was last week; I'll have to send her a *belated* birthday card.
A World War II casualty was given a *belated* Arlington burial on the fortieth anniversary of the war's end.

beleaguer—v.   harass; trouble; besiege
e: The company was pleased to sell its *beleaguered* construction-equipment business.
The *beleaguered* defenders surrendered the fort to the enemy.

belittle—v. to cause to seem little or unimportant, to ridicule

belittlement—n. e: Some parents *belittle* their children constantly.
Do not *belittle* this problem; it could destroy the company.

belly—n. the undersurface or underside; abdomen or stomach
e: The frontier flight made a *belly* landing because its landing gear was not working properly.
Passing through the narrow canal left scratches all along the boat's *belly*.

benign—adj. gentle; kind; not causing serious illness, particularly of a tumor; benevolent; good
e: Some people believe that every *benign*-sounding word that comes out of Moscow is simply public relations.
We were relieved to hear that his tumor was benign.

bereave—v. deprive of, as by death; rob

bereavement—n. e: The prince, *bereaved* since the loss of his wife, has not been able to rule effectively.
Martin Luther King, Jr.'s *bereaved* wife continues to fight to better the conditions for American blacks.

better off—adj. in better condition; in an advantageous position; in comfortable circumstances
e: The president has been arguing that the nation is already *better off* as a result of his policies.
People who live in this expensive part of town are generally much *better off* than those who live in the slums.

bewilder—v. perplex; confuse

bewilderment—n. e: The gunfire all around the soldier *bewildered* him, and he began to shoot at his own men.
I am *bewildered* by these findings—they contradict everything I have heard previously on the subject.

bide—v. remain; wait
e: We *bided* our time by chatting until the meeting resumed.
She *bided* her time until she was reelected, then made her controversial proposal.
"bide one's time"—pass one's time; wait

bilk—v. defraud; cheat; swindle
e: They pleaded guilty of fraud in connection with a scheme in which the company *bilked* various institutions out of large, undisclosed sums of money.
The vice-president was accused of *bilking* the company out of thousands of dollars.

blatant—adj. obvious; clear; obtrusive
e: Helmut Kohl accused the Soviet Union of *blatant* interference in his country's affairs.
Such aggressive acts are *blatantly* in violation of international law.

bleak—adj. pale; barren; gloomy
e: The *bleak* winter weather has kept most people indoors.
The economic forecast was *bleak*, causing the president to worry about his reelection.

blight—n. disease; injury, especially of plants; infestation
blight—v. e: Urban *blight* is a major worry for many city leaders.
The potato crop was *blighted* by a mysterious disease.

blind faith—n. believe without restrictions
e: He has *blind faith* in his program's success, refusing to acknowledge the dangers it raises.
Many put *blind faith* in the power of money, but they may be left emptyhanded after periods of wild inflation.

blindside—v. hit unexpectedly
e: "I have been *blindsided*," said O'Brien, whose store had suddenly been confiscated by a new government policy.
The managers were *blindsided* by the takeover attempt and were helpless to prevent it.

blitz—n. air raid; bombardment; intense campaign
blitz—v. e: The army carried out a massive *blitz* of the area, leaving it unfit for habitation.
In the last few weeks before the election, candidates often use media *blitzes* as a last-ditch effort to capture votes.

blunder—v. make a foolish error; move unsteadily; faux pas; mistake
blunder—n. e: He *blundered* into the wall.
His *blunder* has hurt the company seriously, so he will likely lose his job.

blunt—adj. outspoken; not sharp; insensitive, dull
e: Her *blunt* comments were an embarrassment to the rest of the administration.
October rains have *blunted* earlier enthusiasm for this year's crop.
The public's faith in the president's honesty has increased significantly since last week's speech in which he *bluntly* recognized the difficulties facing the nation.

blush—n. view; appearance; rosiness
e: At first *blush* the reforms seem to be effective, but we must wait for the long term results.
Some things look logical at first *blush* but turn out to be flawed on closer examination.
"at first blush"—when first considered

bluster—v. blow or spark with violence
bluster—n. e: The boss *blustered* at his workers who had not finished their work.
The *blustery* wind blew his hat off and down the block.

bog down—v. cause to sink down; impede
e: The Mafia trials are *bogged* down on a technicality and will be in the courts for months.
In the house, several gas bills seem certain to remain *bogged* down in committee and may never be voted on.

bolster—v. support; build up
e: To slow rising imports, we have *bolstered* the tariffs on selected goods.
Only sound management can *bolster* our profits.

botch—v.   do carelessly or clumsily; ruin; foul up

botchy—adj.   e: The defendant's attorney had simply *botched* the case, losing when his client was clearly innocent.
The project was *botched* up by the new staff members; it will have to be started again from the beginning.

bow—v.   submit; consent (original meaning: bend the body to show respect or submission)

bow—n.   e: The company finally *bowed* to public pressure and cut their waste disposal in half.
Hart has *bowed* out of the campaign because of questions of his personal integrity.
"bow out"—gracefully resign or leave

brace—v.   support; reinforce in preparation; fortify

brace—n.   e: The company *braced* itself for the expected recession by cutting investments.
The army unit *braced* itself for another attack on its position.

breach—n.   infraction or violation of the law; breaking of relations; trespass

breach—v.   e: He was jailed on charges of criminal *breach* of trust.
The builder is being sued for *breach* of contract because not all specifications were followed exactly.

breakthrough—n.   sudden advance; significant accomplishment; discovery
e: Negotiators acknowledged that nothing concrete had been accomplished and that *breakthroughs* were not imminent.
A new *breakthrough* in AIDS research may help prolong the lives of victims.

brew—v.   contrive; ferment, as in beer
e: Although the dictator felt secure, discontent was *brewing* throughout the country.
She was quiet through the entire meeting because a new idea was *brewing* in her mind.

bring about—v.   effect; cause to take place
e: The agreement was formed to *bring about* a peaceful solution to Central America's problems.
The new tax laws are designed to *bring about* a more fair distribution of income.

brisk—adj.   active; lively; sharp; keen
e: The *brisk* wind blew my hat off.
Brisk trading resulted in a steep jump in the price of gold.

bud—n.   undeveloped, incipient, or potential stage (original meaning: beginning of a flower or leaf)
e: "nip in the bud"—stop something in its early stages

bud—v.   e: The new debts nipped the company's bankruptcy in the *bud*, but made its debt problems deeper.
The *budding* space-cargo industry could blossom into a major profitable business.

bulge—n.   curved, swollen part

bulge—v.   e: Iran is still fighting to recover several *bulges* of land that it considers its own.
The guard noticed the large *bulge* in his pocket and suspected he might be carrying a gun.

bullish—adj.　expecting a rise in stock-market prices
　　e: Auto workers were relieved to hear that economists are *bullish* on the American auto industry.
　　Bullish tendencies in the market show that investors are confident about the near future.

bungle—v.　do clumsily; mishandle; ruin
bungler—n.　e: The administration *bungled* into an arms-for-hostages deal with Iran.
　　The ambassador has seriously *bungled* his assignment, straining relations between the two countries.

burgeon—v.　develop rapidly; flourish
　　e: The president decided to stamp out the *burgeoning* opposition movement.
　　Peru's *burgeoning* guerrilla movement becomes more of a threat every day.

burrow—v.　hide or bury oneself
burrow—n.　e: Shultz has *burrowed* himself into an influential but invisible position.
　　The corporation *burrowed* itself into insurmountable debt.

burst—v.　to break open or apart, to shatter
　　e: In a sudden *burst* of emotion, black leaders wept and recalled better days.
　　The police *burst* into the room where the cocaine payoff was taking place.

bustle—n.　noisy; energetic, brisk activity
bustle—v.　e: She was finally able to relax in their summer home, far from the *bustling* of the city.
　　Like most other American towns on the Mexican border, Laredo used to *bustle* with free spending Mexican shoppers.

buttress—v.　support; strengthen
buttress—n.　e: Although these industries do not provide much growth, they do *buttress* the nation's economic foundation.
　　The new evidence *buttressed* their case.

bumper—adj.　bountiful; abundant, especially crops
　　e: Many favorable conditions have led experts to forecast a *bumper* harvest for this year.
　　Rice has long been China's *bumper* crop.

CHAPTER II

C–D WORDS

chafe—v. irritate; become irritated, aggravate
  e: The senator's wife *chafed* at the accusation that her husband drank heavily.
  The labor party *chafed* in opposition to the proposal for deunionization.

chagrin—n. embarrassment; humiliation
  e: Much to the *chagrin* of the host, the meal was badly burned.
  Chagrined members of the delegation discovered their proposal was based on a false set of data.

chair—v. preside over a meeting
chairman—n. e: The head of the board *chaired* the annual stockholders' meeting.
  Williams *chairs* the treasury department meetings.

chalk up—v. score; earn; credit
  e: The stock market has *chalked up* large gains in recent weeks.
  The democrats chalked up a mid-term victory in November.

chary—adj. careful; wary; cautious
chariness—n. e: U.S. officials were *chary* of discussing details of the arms talks until the meetings were over.
  Due to the recent scandals, he is *chary* of being seen in public with any woman except his wife or his mother.

chastise—v. criticize; punish; scold
chastisement—n.
chasten—v. e: The ambassador was dismissed from his post as *chastisement* for his poor diplomacy.
  The opposition has *chastised* the president's inflexible position on the Star Wars defense system.

chide—v.   scold; rebuke; reprimand
   e: The U.S. has *chided* its major trading partners for not stimulating their economies.
   The prime minister has been *chided* for refusing to take a stand on international terrorism.

choke off—v.   terminate; block up
   e: The current economic recovery could be *choked off* by the growing deficits.
   Rising mortgage interest rates may *choke off* recent home buying.
   origin: choke—to prevent someone's breathing

churn out—v.   produce mechanically; grind out
   e: Japan would be threatened if the U.S. started *churning out* engineers instead of lawyers.
   The computer should *churn out* the results of the survey within minutes.
   origin: churn—large container in which milk is stirred to make butter

circumvent—v.   avoid; overcome; bypass
circumvention—n.   e: It takes little effort to *circumvent* government control over these local housing projects.
   The manager was a master at *circumventing* the standard tiresome procedures.

cleft—n.   split; fissure
cleft—adj.   e: The *cleft* between rich and poor nations is growing wider.
   Our country's progress has been slowed by the constant *cleft* between opposing parties.

clip—v.   cut off; crop; reduce
   e: The recent trend toward protectionism has *clipped* exports dramatically.
   Some benefits must be *clipped* from the proposed contract before the management will agree to it.

closure—n.   act of closing
   e: Major steel producers offered voluntary *closures* in exchange for protective tariffs.
   The deal's *closure* depends on whether or not enough funds can be raised on time.

cluster—v.   collect; make a bunch or group; assemble
cluster—n.   e: The civilians *clustered* in bomb shelters as war planes rained bombs down on their heads.
   Prices on new compact cars *cluster* around twelve thousand dollars.

cocky—adj.   overly self-confident; showy; conceited
   e: The new manager, *cocky* and quick-tongued, soon annoyed all of his staff.
   Her *cocky* attitude made her well-known in Parliament, but won her few friends.
   origin: cock—male bird

concede—v.   acknowledge as true or proper
concession—n.   e: The president *conceded* that his plan would not immediately boost the unemployment rate.
   When it became clear that his opponent was sure to win, he gracefully *conceded* the race.
   "concede an election"—accept defeat; acknowledge the victory of one's opponent

11

conceal—v.   keep from discovery; hide

concealment—n.   e: He evaded capture and entered the U.S. in 1956 after *concealing* his Nazi past.

The thieves had entered the bank with guns *concealed* in their heavy coats.

concoct—v.   invent; falsify; create

concoction—n.   e: The jury did not believe that he had not played any role in *concocting* the diaries.

The governor and the accused aides were allowed to resign behind the cover of a *concocted* story.

condone—v.   approve of; overlook; forgive

e: He denied that he had *condoned* an arms shipment by Israel.

We cannot *condone* such behavior from an employee; he will have to be fired.

confer—v.   discuss; bring together

conference—n.   e: The ministers have *conferred* at length with the new president to inform him of recent developments.

Today the board *conferred* on the problem of growing competition.

contempt—n.   bitter scorn

contemptible—adj.

contemptuous—adj.   e: A march for democracy drew tens of thousands to the presidential palace to shout their *contempt* of the ruling armed forces.

The House voted to hold the EPA administrator in *contempt* of Congress for withholding information.

"contempt of court"—disrespect or disobedience shown to a court

contrive—v.   devise; manage; plan

contrivance—n.   e: The peace talks were *contrived* to cover up great defense spending increases.

The Soviets criticized the U.S.-Mideast Plan as *contrivance* with Israel.

convene—v.   assemble; meet; congregate

convention—n.   e: The Senate *convened* for what it hoped would be the last session of the year.

A hearing was *convened* to discuss the town's bond issuance.

counter—v.   oppose; counterdemand

counter—adj.   e: Companies have had to lower prices to *counter* subsidized foreign export.

His debating skills were obvious as he *countered* every argument his opponent raised.

coy—adj.   devious; turning; twisted; shy

e: His *coy* comments convinced us that he was secretly working against the party.

She *coyly* mentioned that big changes could be coming, but she refused to elaborate.

craving—n.   longing; yearning; desiring

crave—v.   e: The increasing *craving* for Japanese electronics has prevented a lowering of trade deficits.

It is obvious that she only *craves* power and has no real interest in the voters.

creep—v. develop or advance by slow degrees, crawl

e: In some periods we must be prepared to tolerate a certain degree of *creeping* inflation.

Prices are *creeping* up to their predepression state.

crony—n. old companion; friend; pal

e: One of his former employees accused him of hiring mostly *cronies* and girlfriends.

He is an old *crony* of the premier and should not be touched by the purges.

cull—v. select; choose

e: He *culled* his data from many sources.

She *culled* her thoughts before writing them down.

dabble—v. undertake superficially

dabbler—n. e: She used her extra income to *dabble* in the stock market.

He *dabbles* in many diverse endeavors in his spare time.

dash—v. break; smash;

e: This month's disappointing figures *dashed* hopes for a general economic recovery in Europe.

The possibility of an agreement was *dashed* by their sudden refusal to compromise.

dearth—n. lack; absence; scarcity

e: There was a *dearth* of news from the war zone.

Our *dearth* of knowledge about East Asia puts us at a disadvantage when doing business there.

deceptive—adj. misleading; tending to deceive; false

deceive—v.

deception—n. e: If inflation is ignored, the deficits are *deceptively* large.

It is hard to trust her because in the past she has been so *deceptive*.

decline—v. refuse; decrease

decline—n. e: The *decline* in Arab oil earnings has lead to the weakening of their cartel.

The minister refused to answer questions about his personal affairs.

decoy—n. false sign meant to lure; inducement; attract

decoy—v. e: The frontal attack was only a *decoy* to hide the main attack from behind.

This motorcade is a *decoy* to confuse would-be assassins; the president entered town last night.

deed—n. action; act; accomplishment

e: He describes the explosion as a cowardly, criminal *deed*.

At the man's funeral, the speaker praised the many honorable *deeds* he had done for his country.

deed—n. A document sealed as an instrument of bond, contract, or conveyance (usually pertaining to property); title

deed—v. e: In his father's will he inherited the *deed* to the family home.

After receiving the buyer's check, he sent her the *deed* to the car.

deft—adj.   skillful, expert
e: The likable chairman has *deftly* managed to form a new coalition.
A true politician, he *deftly* handled even the most difficult questions at the press conference.

defuse—v.   make less tense
e: Seeking to *defuse* the budget controversy, war propaganda was increased.
The reassuring speeches by world leaders helped to *defuse* an international crisis.
origin: fuse—line leading to a bomb

delude—v.   deceive; trick; mislead
delusion—n.
delusive—adj.   e: Although reconfirming his commitment to continued negotiations, the president said, "We should not *delude* ourselves into expecting an agreement soon."
Don't be *deluded* by his fancy talk—his project is not worth the investment.

delve—v.   search; explore
e: The initial findings have been fruitful, so we will *delve* further into the matter.
By *delving* into the killer's thoughts, the psychologist was able to discover his true motive.

demote—v.   reduce in rank, grade, or position
demotion—n.   e: Officials proven unqualified for their positions will be *demoted* or transferred.
The chief threatened to *demote* him to captain because he often ignored approved procedures.

dent—v.   alter; change slightly; bend
dent—n.   e: The complexity of market experience has *dented* these simple economic models.
The country's 1 million tons of sugar are insignificant; they hardly make a *dent* in the world's market.
origin: dent—hit causing slight depression

deride—v.   ridicule; speak with scoff; mock
derision—n.
derisive—adj.   e: Some officers *deride* this account of the story insisting that it is simply impossible.
The young councilman was *derided* for proposing such impractical solutions.

despicable—adj.   worthless; contemptible; detest
despise—v.   e: Your behavior is *despicable* and unsuitable for a diplomat.
We recommend the death penalty for killers so *despicable* that they can never reform.

desultory—n.   progressing aimlessly
e: The *desultory* hourlong conversations were of no use in progressing toward a contract settlement.
Thompson has made some *desultory* efforts to return to practicing law, but she has not yet tried seriously.

14

deter—v.   prevent; discourage; divert
deterrence—n.
deterrent—adj.
determent—n.   e: Chronic political instability creates uncertainty, which *deters* longterm investment.
Will a U.S. nuclear buildup *deter* the Soviets from expanding their sphere of influence?

devoid—adj.   empty; void; deficient
e: He is so upset that he is *devoid* of all reason.
He expected that the panel's statement would be *devoid* of criticisms of his conduct.

diminution—n.   lessening; detraction; decrease; reduce
diminutive—adj.
diminish—v.
diminishment—n.   e: The president refused to accept legislation that would lead to a *diminution* of his power.
Recent *diminution* of public support has become a major worry for the White House.

dire—adj.   dreadful; frightening; desperate
e: Geologists have repeatedly issued *dire* warnings about a major California earthquake.
The country's *dire* economic plight helped to fuel the revolution.

disgruntle—v.   cause to become disappointed or angry
e: Running such an impersonal business will only *disgruntle* your customers.
Disgruntled supporters of the orchestra have threatened to remove their support unless the new conductor is replaced.

disheveled—adj.   disarranged or disordered; messy
dishevelment—n.
dishevel—v.   e: More and more dirty, *disheveled* people can be seen wandering the streets of America's big cities.
The congressman emerged after the thirty-six hour marathon session, *disheveled* but triumphant.

dislodge—v.   remove; drive out from a dwelling place; displace
e: They used all kind of forces to *dislodge* the rebels from their position in the hills.
In the latest purges, Wang was *dislodged* from his protected position in the local government.
origin: "lodge"—stay in a rented room

dismal—adj.   disastrous; marked as unlucky; discouraging
e: The possibility of the president's budget cuts being accepted appears *dismal* because his usual supporters have all spoken out against them.

disparage—v.   reduce; minimize; ridicule
disparagement—n.   e: The Soviets *disparaged* the U.S. grain offer, saying that they would rely on other sources.
You should refrain from making such *disparaging* remarks about your superiors.

dispel—v.   drive out; disperse
e: In order to *dispel* any doubts concerning his financial affairs, the vice-president has

15

made his tax return public.

Her powerful speech in Parliament has *dispelled* reservations of her leadership abilities.

dissemble—v.   disguise the real nature of; simulate; camouflage
  e: the leaders are done with *dissembling* their intentions to maintain superpower support.
  He was attacked for his *dissembling* and misleading testimony.

distort—v.   alter misleadingly; deceive
distortion—n.   e: Democrats have charged that the president has distorted the figures on the U.S.-Soviet nuclear-arms balance.
  If we ignore historical factors, we will get a *distorted* picture of the leaders' intentions.

ditch—v.   discard; abandon; canal; trench
  e: Three robbery suspects tried to *ditch* the evidence by flinging hundreds of dollars out the car window.
  Falling sales have forced the company to *ditch* plans to build a second plant.

divest—v.   deprive; disinvest
divestiture—n.   e: He resisted pressure to join those favoring *divestiture* of South African stock.
  The political prisoners have been *divested* of all basic human rights.

dogged—adj.   stubborn; tenacious; determined
doggedness—n.   e: Japanese success is the result of the willingness to work *doggedly*.
  I will fight my way to the top as *doggedly* as any other politician!

doldrums—n.   period of inactivity or depression
  e: Strong business activity is badly needed to break out of the *doldrums* of recession.
  She has been in the *doldrums* since her defeat in a try for the U.S. Senate.

dolt—n.   idiot; imbecile; fool
doltish—adj.   e: The great importance placed on presenting a good public image has led some to comment that only *dolts* enter government.
  How can he expect to run a serious campaign when all his workers are such *dolts*?

doom—v.   condemn; ruin; destine
doom—n.   e: An attempt to rid the economy of inflation is *doomed* if the present destructive policies are continued.
  Her political career was *doomed* when the story of her drug use hit the newspapers.

dot—v.   appear randomly and numerously; point; mark
  e: Wall Street's firmament is being *dotted* by increasing numbers of fledgling companies.
  Resort towns *dot* the beautiful coastline.

dote—v.   show excessive fondness; spoil
doter—n.   e: The way he *dotes* upon the boss is sickening.
She was a quiet young woman who had been *doted* upon by her father.

douse—v.   soak; extinguish
e: Between now and next month's election, the different parties will *douse* each other with insults.
The fire was finally *doused* with the help of two neighboring fire departments.

draft—v.   design; represent; compose; sketch
draft—n.   e: The original *draft* of the arms proposal was over one hundred pages long.
The will is a complicated one and must be *drafted* by a skilled lawyer.

dread—v.   feel fear or anxiety; distrust
dread—n.
dreadful—adj.   e: He lived *dreading* that his wife would find out about his affair with his secretary.
She was beginning to *dread* seeing her boss because every time she did she was piled with more work.

dredge up—v.   dig up; pull out; gather
e: All this happened a year ago, and I *dredge* it *up* only for its broader relevance.
He puts his staff to work *dredging up* information on his opponent.
origin: "dredge"—remove soil from a body of water.

drove—n.   group of animals driven or moved, group of people moving or acting together.
e: *Droves* of peasants stormed into the city; the revolution had begun.
The locusts came in *droves*, destroying crops for miles.

drum up—v.   summon; originate; gather
e: Syria is trying to *drum up* internal resistance to the tentative agreement.
He has been unable to *drum up* enough support and will drop out of the race.

dud—n.   bomb that fails to explode; something that is disappointingly unsuccessful
e: Some innovations turn out to be *duds*, he explained, predicting that automatic banking machines would not catch on.
All the bombs delivered in the arms deal turned out to be *duds*.

CHAPTER III

E–F WORDS

ebb—v. decline; diminish
ebb—n. e: The shift reflects the Germans' growing optimism about their economy and *ebbing* concern over U.S. interest rates.
The war continues to heat up; serious fighting has not *ebbed* for the winter.
origin: "ebb"—receding tides

edge—n. advantage; upper hand; border
e: In most technological fields, we have a substantial *edge* on the Soviets.
Her inside information was the *edge* she needed to win the contract.
The steep daily fluctuations in the stock market have kept the whole financial world on *edge*.
"on edge"—tense; nervous

edgy—adj. sharp; tense; irritable; nervous
edginess—n. e: The rapid changes in the economy have left many businessmen nervous and *edgy* lately.
She had been *edgy* every day until the contract was signed.

effect—v. accomplish; perform; result
effect—n. e: The long-term *effects* of exposure to radiation are still not understood.
The movie *E.T.* used many special *effects*.

effrontery—n. boldness; shamelessness
e: I do not believe they will have the *effrontery* to insult the prime minister publicly.
Confronted with such *effrontery*, the delegation had no choice but to walk out of the meeting.

egregious—adj. distinguished; flagrant; deplorable
egregiousness—n. e: Despite his *egregious* error, we accepted him as a member of the panel.
My accountant made an *egregious* error on my taxes, costing me hundreds.

elation—n.   extreme happiness; delight

elate—v.   e: Post editors and reporters greeted yesterday's decision to continue publication with *elation*.

Other problems were forgotten amid the *elation* over the end of the war.

embezzlement—n.   theft, cheat

embezzle—v.

embezzler—n.   e: The bishop was being tried for *embezzlement* of church funds.

Over three months she was able to *embezzle* thousands from the company before anyone noticed.

embroil—v.   become deeply involved

embroilment—n.   e: The SUF *embroils* itself in the most volatile issues of domestic politics.

It seems the two countries will be *embroiled* in conflict indefinitely.

enact—v.   legalize; establish

enactment—n.

enactor—n.   e: The tax cut was *enacted* on July 1.

The *enactment* of laws against racial segregation has taken a step toward bettering the position of blacks in America.

encroach—v.   intrude; trespass; invade

encroachment—n.   e: Party cadres resist changes that would *encroach* on their power.

The ever-growing city *encroached* upon the peaceful countryside.

encumber—v.   hinder; weigh down; impede

encumbrance—n.   e: Leaders in all parts of the world are fighting the growing bureaucracies that have *encumbered* their efforts.

Costly regulation has *encumbered* American business.

endow—v.   enrich; credit; confer

endowment—n.   e: The present market tends to support the well-*endowed* and hinder the poor.

Ivy League schools are among the best-*endowed* in the country.

endue—v.   provide with

e: She is young and *endued* with a desire for high achievement.

Her rigorous education has *endued* her with exacting analytical skills.

endure—v.   tolerate; bear; abide

endurable—adj.

endurance—n.   e: One has to *endure* many hardships during one's life.

New companies often cannot *endure* hard economic times.

enfeeble—v.   weaken; make feeble

enfeeblement—n.   e: These regulations will help a few companies, but *enfeeble* the economy's overall efficiency.

Her body was slowly *enfeebled* by the crippling disease.

enjoin—v.   forbid; command, advise

enjoinder—n.   e: The court *enjoined* the jury from public contact concerning the case.

The states have been *enjoined* to get tougher on speeding or lose federal highway funds.

ensue—v.   follow as a result; immediately following

ensuing—adj.   e: The committee met to set federal monetary policy for the *ensuing* months.

The earthquake killed ten; the *ensuing* panic cost an additional eight lives.

entice—v.   attract by arousing hope or desire; lure; tempt

enticement—n.   e: Foreign money flowed into the country, *enticed* by the prospect of steadily climbing oil revenues.

Enticed by the possibility of quick profits, she wasted her money on an ill-planned project.

entrepreneur—n.   one who organizes or innovates; businessman

enterpreneurial—adj.   e: Washington has turned its wage-increasing toward the *entrepreneurs* as the nation's last hope for economic revival.

An *enterpreneurial* spirit is necessary for economic development.

equate—v.   regard as equal; compare

equation—n.   e: They were worried by fluctuations in the fledgling economy, *equating* economic trouble with political turmoil.

Some analysts *equate* the Soviet Union with the United States in terms of foreign policy.

err—v.   deviate from proper aim; fail

erroneously—adj.

error—n.

errant—adj.   e: Critics say the U.S. *erred* in refusing to sell grain to the Soviets because they merely bought it from other countries.

The accountants *erred* in calculating operating expenses, which led to serious financial mismanagement.

escape hatch—n.   opening that allows one to escape or get free

e: The submarines' *escape hatches* were all found to be defective, which led to protests from the sailors.

By never being actively involved in the drug deals, she allowed herself an *escape hatch* in case they were discovered.

estranged—adj.   disaffected; alienated

estrangement—n.   e: He has been *estranged* from the revolution because he has no friends on either side.

The recent summit appears to have moved the two regional giants from past *estrangement* toward cooperation.

evil—n.   harm; something bringing sorrow or distress; profane; corrupt

e: The notion prevails that inflation and unemployment are two *evils* that can be conveniently traded for one another.

excise tax—n.   duty on home goods

e: Japanese cars are now subject to an *excise tax* to try to slow domestic consumption.

States frequently impose an *excise tax* on alcoholic beverages.

excludable—adj. subject to exclusion; ban

exclusion—n.

exclude—v.

exclusive—adj. e: The federal government must grant *excludable* aliens some of the constitutional safeguards enjoyed by American citizens.

The *exclusion* of blacks from an apartment house may be illegal, but is certainly not uncommon.

exempt—v. release from obligation; excuse

exemptible—adj.

exemption—n.

exempt—adj. e: The ordinance *exempts* only hotel restaurants from being prohibited to serve alcoholic drinks late at night.

He has declared himself *exempt* from paying taxes, since he will not make much money this year.

extol—v. praise; glorify; celebrate

e: The manager *extolled* the virtues of his company to prospective investors.

The top salesman was *extolled* for his aggressive style.

falter—v. hesitate; show unsteadiness

e: Gulf oil ministers met to discuss how to prop up *faltering* prices.

The *faltering* economy leaves everyone unsure of whether or not to invest now.

famine—n. extreme food shortage; dearth

famished—adj. e: *Famine* swept through Ireland in the 1980s.

The *famine* in Africa continues, even though relief money is becoming scarce.

fan—v. stimulate; stir up; booster

e: She complained that every step to ease martial law had only met with the *fanning* of tensions.

The increasingly common shortages *fanned* the flames of rebellion among the people.

origin: fan—object used to create a breeze.

fare—v. get along; succeed; experience

e: The administration appears to be *faring* better in the Senate because of the greater proportion of loyal Republicans.

The Dow Jones industrial average *fared* rather well today, up 11.3 points.

fealty—n. loyalty; feudal allegiance

e: This town falls within the duke's domain; they are the *fealty* to him.

One by one he made them pledge their *fealty* to him.

feat—n. achievement; accomplishment

e: The newspapers refer to the recovery of the failing industry as a *feat* of brilliant management.

Many believed Reagan's victory in 1980 was quite a *feat* for someone his age.

fend off—v. defend; struggle against; ward

e: The British Steel Company is trying to *fend off* import duties to subsidized steel it sells in the U.S.

The Palestinians *fended off* repeated Israeli attacks.

fetter—v.   chain; shackle
fetter—n.   e: The economy has been *fettered* by too much regulation.
The present regime has *fettered* the people for forty years, and there is no reason to believe they will be freed.

fickle—adj.   changeable; inconstant; erratic
fickleness—n.   e: Congress's *fickle* budget-control process has destroyed the confidence of the business world.
The president has complained that Europe has been too *fickle* in its support of U.S. policies.

filibuster—n.   delaying tactics; especially giving lengthy speeches to delay legislation.
filibuster—v.   e: Opponents of the bill appear ready to resist at length, even *filibuster*, on the Senate floor.
The Senate has been locked in a *filibuster* for days and has not been able to get to the important issues on its agenda.

fizzle out—v.   fail gradually; die out
e: Manufacturers are cutting back production as heavy buying from the recovery *fizzles out*.
The plan to build a new plant has *fizzled out* as funds cannot be raised in time.

flabbergast—v.   overwhelm with astonishment; astound; amaze
e: Family and friends were *flabbergasted* by his sudden decision to withdraw from the presidential race.
Onlookers watched *flabbergasted* as he pulled out a gun and shot the bank teller.

flamboyant—adj.   showy; flashy; ostentatious
flamboyance—n.   e: Edwards, the *flamboyant* chief executive, has ordered a private helicopter for himself.
The leader's *flamboyance*, instead of annoying the voters, has only made him more popular.

flare-up—n.   sudden growth or outburst
flare up—v.   e: It appears to be the worst *flare-up* of fighting in the eleven-year conflict.
A deteriorating business outlook has reduced the risks of a *flare-up* in interest rates.

flashy—adj.   superficially impressive; showy; dazzling
e: He likes to invest in *flashy* foreign operations, though many of them are not especially profitable.
He bought a *flashy* new sports car to impress the women in his office.

flaunt—v.   parade; show vainly; exhibit
e: She has a flamboyant style of living and she likes to *flaunt* it in front of her colleagues.
He threw a big party at his country estate to *flaunt* his riches to his friends.

fledgling—adj.   undeveloped; inexperienced
fledgling—n.   e: Many *fledgling* companies are given special tax breaks to help them get started.
She was still a *fledgling* among veterans, but she was beginning to earn their respect.

flinch—v.   shrink away in pain or fear; shiver
flinch—n.   e: He did not *flinch* as he was sentenced to prison because he knew it was inevitable.
The senator has changed his loyalties with this vote, *flinching* from the pressure building from voters in his state.

flippant—adj.   disrespectful; frivolous
e: This is an issue of war and peace and must not be treated so *flippantly*.
His continually *flippant* answers annoyed the judge intensely.

flock—n.   group of animals or people
flock—v.   e: Ministers speak to their fathered *flocks* about the coming of the Lord.
Shepherds killed their *flocks* for meat rather than turn them over to the government.

flog—v.   beat severely; scourge
e: A few hundred years ago public *flogging* was an acceptable way to punish criminals.
Student protesters complain of being *flogged* by riot police.

flounder—v.   act awkwardly and aimlessly; collapse, hesitate
flounderer—n.   e: For the last year the company has been selling properties to keep from *floundering*.
In recent months, attempts to restore OPEC unity have *floundered* as disagreements are multiplying.

flout—v.   show contempt or scorn for; mock; ridicule
flout—n.   e: *Flouting* the wise resolutions of the committee, the new chairman has decided to do things his own way.
The latest protests in the street have been interpreted as simply attempts to *flout* the law.

fluke—n.   unexpected stroke of good luck; miracle
fluky—adj.   e: The supposed drop in the crime rate had been a statistical *fluke* caused by the change of calculating procedures.
It was merely a *fluke* of birth that she had been born into such a rich family.

flurry—n.   sudden burst of activity
flurry—v.   e: Contract negotiations broke down yesterday after a *flurry* of charges from both sides.
Lewi's departure was an isolated event and not the start of a *flurry* of cabinet-level shifts.

fodder—n.   animal feed; basic essentials
e: During the famine, that which was usually used as *fodder* was highly sought after.
There also is the *fodder* for a regional political debate.

foe—n.   enemy; adversary
e: The president's main *foes* in the opposition party have disappeared mysteriously at night.
He is an able *foe* in fencing.

23

fog—n.   confusion; haze; daze
fogginess—n.
foggy—adj.
fog—v. e: We hope the debate can avoid becoming *fogged* in political and emotional rhetoric.
Most of the protesters in the streets had only a *foggy* idea of what they wanted.
origin: fog—cloudlike mist near the ground that lessens visibility

fond—adj.   affectionate; tender
fondness—n. e: They *fondly* embrace when dealing with members of their organization.
The governor's present troubles will make him remember his preelection days with *fondness*.

foray—n.   raid, as for plunder; attack
foray—v. e: The territory to the north has served as a launching point for some rebel *forays*.
Rebel forces have been growing in strength and have stepped up *forays* throughout the country.

foreclosure—n.   deprivation of possessions, usually for failure to repay a loan
foreclose—v. e: A Kensington homeowner lost a court battle to stop a *foreclosure* on his home mortgage.
Because of the depressed economic situation local banks have been forced into more *foreclosures* than ever before.

foreshadow—v.   represent or indicate beforehand; prefigure
foreshadowing—n. e: The chaotic events of the day *foreshadowed* the disaster.
The latest stock-market jump was *foreshadowed* by this year's steady growth in GNP.

forestall—v.   prevent; anticipate; deter
e: Rather than go into bankruptcy, they have *forestalled* all payments until next year.
The Federal Reserve Board has been trying to *forestall* a recession by keeping interest rates low.

foretell—v.   predict; forecast; divine
e: Despite all the present discussion, no one seems able to *foretell* what the economy will do in the next few months.
Her decisive victory in the election seems to *foretell* a bright political career.

forfeit—v.   lose, give up; default
forfeiture—n.
forfeit—n. e: They agreed to *forfeit* ten thousand dollars in profits because of their illegal dumping of chemicals.
The court ruling lists several properties subject to *forfeiture* to the government.

foster—v.   bring up; encourage; nourish
e: Not one economics professor at the university believes that instability *fosters* prosperity.
The latest fine tuning by the federal reserve is designed to *foster* a healthy economic recovery.

franchise—n.　privilege or right, especially the right to vote

e: The country's chief executive has been elected through universal *franchise*.
Only recently has the *franchise* been extended to women.

fraught—adj.　accompanied; being full of

e: I find it difficult to support a strategy so *fraught* with risks.
The road before us is *fraught* with danger, but we must have the courage to walk it.

fray—n.　dispute; noisy quarrel; ravel; commotion
fray—v.　e: The spectators joined in the *fray* on the playing field.
The mayor cleared the public out of the city council room in order to avoid a *fray*.

frenzy—n.　temporary mental or emotional agitation
frenzied—adj.　e: Construction workers are building at a *frenzied* pace to try to meet next
month's deadline.
The young lawyer was in a *frenzy* over his first court appearance, and had to be calmed
by an older member of the firm.

fretful—adj.　irritable; tending to worry
fret—v.　e: Administration officials seem to becoming *fretful* as every economic sign is
predicting a severe recession.
I've hired an assistant manager who *frets* over day-to-day problems for me.

fruition—n.　accomplishment; enjoyment; fulfillment
fruitful—adj.
fruitless—adj.　e: He contacted several big newspapers hoping to use them to tell his
side of the story, but nothing came to *fruition*.
origin: fruit—fleshy, edible growth on trees

funnel—v.　move; cause to move

e: The Soviet Union and its allies are *funneling* military equipment into Nicaragua.
He engineered a plan to *funnel* proceeds from Iranian arm sales to the contras.
origin: funnel—cone-shaped utensil that facilitates pouring liquids or powders into
small-mouthed containers

furlough—v.　lay off from work
furlough—n.　e: The Internal Revenue Service told its employees that they will be *fur-
loughed* involuntarily because there is no money to pay their salaries.
The threatened *furlough* of employees at the IRS was temporarily averted late yesterday.

CHAPTER IV

G–H WORDS

gall—v. exasperate; make angry
e: The strong contradiction between what she says and what she does is *galling*.
It *galls* me to have to listen to my boss when I know I could be doing a better job than he does.

gape—v. stare
e: The politician *gaped* in embarrassment as his wife fainted on the stage.
A crowd of people stood *gaping* helplessly at the man caught in the burning high-rise.

gender gap—n. differences between the sexes
e: One example of the *gender-gap* phenomenon is that women vote in greater numbers than men.
Thousands of women gathered in Washington to protest what they see as a growing *gender gap*.

ghastly—adj. frightening; very unpleasant
e: The company was prospering until her partner left the country with the company funds, a truly *ghastly* turn of events.
The defendant's expression was positively *ghastly* as she described how her husband beat her.
origin: ghost—spirit; soul

gibe—v. make mocking remarks
e: The two boxers exchanged well-rehearsed *gibes* on television to promote their upcoming fight.
The assistant manager is often *gibed* by his co-workers for being excessively friendly to the boss.

gimmick—n. trick; attention-getting strategy
gimmickry—n. e: The press has been speculating that the recent focus on social issues was just a political *gimmick* to raise government expenditures.
Some economists assert that supply-side economics is a *gimmick* and a slogan to allow the Reagan administration to overspend.

gingerly—adv.   cautiously
 e: The failure of complete central planning seems to have shocked the regime into *gingerly* embarking on moderation.
 Reagan has *gingerly* agreed to raise taxes, despite his previous statements that he never would.

gleam—n.   flash; glint
gleam—v.   e: The mayor, well known as a family man, speaks of his children with a *gleam* in his eye.
 The current rise in the price of tin offers a *gleam* of hope for economically depressed Bolivia, as tin is one of its major exports.

glib—adj.   fluent; easy with speech
 e: The former senator, a recognized expert, spoke *glibly* on the issue of economic solidarity.
 She has proven herself to be a *glib* spokeswoman for the department of defense.

glimmer—n.   flash; spark; hint
glimmer—v.   e: The announcement of a meeting between the two countries' leaders offers a *glimmer* of hope for a peaceful resolution of their border dispute.
 What he said is all lies; it contains not even a *glimmer* of truth.

gloomy—adj.   depressed; sullen
gloomily—adv.
gloom—n.   e: This month's depressing economic figures paint a *gloomy* picture for the near future.
 The *gloomy* weather continued for over a week before the sun finally appeared.

gloss over—v.   treat superficially; intending to detract attention from a fault or problem
 e: In his usual, direct way, Mr. Reagan made no attempt to *gloss over* the deep difficulties facing the arms negotiators.
 Her report was criticized for *glossing over* several important issues.

grapple—v.   wrestle; struggle
 e: Latin American countries have offered a new set of proposals to *grapple* with the debt problem.
 The president has been *grappling* with an uncooperative legislature since he took office.

gripe—v.   grumble; complain
gripe—n.   e: The boss does not listen to the *gripes* of his employees.
 The governor dismissed opposition to his program as "the *griping* of special interest."

grist—n.   matter of interest or value
 e: Its findings are sure to serve as *grist* for criminal investigations.
 origin: grist—grain to be ground

grudge—n.   resentment; rancor
grudge—v.   e: President Reagan said that he bears no *grudge* against the man who shot him.
 Those who have angered Robertson have found that he can hold a *grudge* for years.

gut—v.   destroy the inside of

    e: Britain announced the loss of the frigate *Antelope*, which sank after it was *gutted* by fire from Argentine bombing raids.

    The building was *gutted* five years ago and has remained out of use ever since.

hack—n.   cut roughly
hack—v.   e: The murdered man's body was found to have been *hacked* all over with a large knife.

    Yesterday a councillor in Johannesburg was *hacked* to death by an angry mob.

hail—v.   praise; salute
hail—n.   e: His program has been *hailed* by conservatives, who are happy with the proposed spending cuts.

    The army band played "*Hail* to the Chief" as Bush entered the auditorium.

hamlet—n.   small village

    e: She was born in a *hamlet*, but moved to Paris to search for a more exciting life.

    In contrast to the violence in the capitol, the *hamlets* of the south have remained quite peaceful.

hammer out—v.   work out; strike a deal

    e: Israel's cabinet accepted the agreement that was *hammered out* yesterday.

    Many key points remain to be *hammered out* before an arms agreement can be reached.

    origin: hammer—tool for pounding

hamstring—v.   make ineffective or powerless

    e: Aides say the president is unable to reform the economy as he is being increasingly *hamstrung* by his party critics.

    Spokesmen for the auto industry complain that they are *hamstrung* by excessive safety and pollution regulations.

    origin: hamstring—vital tendon of the leg

handout—n.   donation given to poor

    e: At Christmastime more people than usual help to provide *handouts* to the poor.

    The press has been suggesting that the new subsidies to the garment industry are simply *handouts* to Senator Davis's supporters.

hardship—n.   suffering; deprivation

    e: In diplomatic circles all assignments to communist countries are considered *hardship* posts.

    The *hardships* of living in Northern Canada prove too difficult for the common man.

harp on—v.   discourse relentlessly on a subject; discuss excessively

    e: In response to U.S. criticism of Europe's sale of pipeline equipment to the USSR, France is *harping on* the fact that the U.S. sells grains to them.

    Management has been *harping* on worker laziness lately, further aggravating the already tense negotiations.

harrow—v.   distress; torment

e: His ex-wife, sometimes sobbing, gave crucial testimony against him for three *harrowing* hours.

He still remembers almost drowning as a child as the most *harrowing* experience of his life.

origin: harrow—tool used to break up soil

harsh—adj.   painful; severe; cruel

harshness—n. e: The *harshness* of the recession, in part, reflected American firms adjusting to meet foreign competition.

The *harsh* climate of the Tibetan plateau has made the people tough enough to survive anywhere.

hasten—v.   urge on; accelerate

hastiness—n.

hasty—adj.

haste—n. e: The replacement of old machinery with modern equipment has *hastened* the growth of the company.

Critics asserted that negotiators had acted *hastily* in accepting the present ceasefire agreement.

hatch—v.   devise; formulate

e: A plan was *hatched* to rob the partner of his money.

Ortega accused the U.S. of *hatching* a scheme to spread dissension in his country.

origin: hatch—an animal's young breaking out of its egg.

haunt—v.   reappear; persist

haunt—n. e: Another worry is beginning to *haunt* some Lebanese: the inability of the economy to show any signs of growth.

Argentina continues to be *haunted* by the issue of the six thousand people who died mysteriously in the village near the chemical factory.

origin: haunt—to visit as a ghost

havoc—n.   devastation; disorder

e: The sudden change in the exchange rates plays *havoc* with my plans to increase foreign investment.

The flooding in the northwest has wreaked *havoc* for the farmers there.

"play havoc with," "wreak havoc"—ruin; devastate

hawker—n.   one that sells wares; street seller

hawk—v. e: Taxi drivers and street *hawkers* form syndicates to play the market.

Hawkers are once again appearing on the streets, a sign of stability after the weeks of citywide violence.

heady—adj.   stubborn; willful

e: The general manager's *heady* decision-making angered everyone who worked with him.

His campaign was damaged by the *heady* remarks from his campaign manager.

heckler—n.   person harassing a speaker with questions or comments

heckle—v.   e: The president was interrupted in mid-speech by a *heckler* protesting his South African policy.

Rebels say they did not take lightly the *heckling* of the Pope by Sandinistas.

heed—n.   attention; notice

heed—v.

heedful—adj.

heedless—adj.   e: The warning given by the stock-market crash must be *heeded*.

The president has been careful about dealing with local leaders, as the people generally *heed* what they say.

heel—v.   follow closely or subserviently

heel—n.   e: Gold's price dropped yesterday on the *heels* of a sharp gain the day before.

Much progress has been made in bringing inflation to *heel*.

origin: heel—rounded, back part of the foot

"on the heels of"—closely following

"bring to heel"—subdue; conquer

hefty—adj.   substantial; powerful

heft—n.

heft—v.   e: The company's growing profits have meant *hefty* raises for all levels of management.

Inflation showed a *hefty* jump in October, causing speculation of an ensuing recession.

henchman—n.   trusted follower

e: The president accused the Soviets and their *henchmen* in Havana of spreading repression.

Some of Capelli's *henchmen* have been brought to trial, but the boss has escaped any accusation.

hesitate—v.   avoid action or decision

hesitancy—n.

hesitation—n.

hesitant—adj.   e: The prime minister blamed the import restrictions of his country's trading partners for his *hesitancy* in pursuing free trade.

Observers see the mayor's *hesitancy* to use force against the protesters as a fatal mistake.

hiatus—n.   break; gap

e: The senator returned to politics after a two-year *hiatus* to improve his declining health.

The chairman appeared in public again today after a *hiatus* of three weeks.

hike—n.   sudden rise; increase

e: The pay *hikes* would not be given if economic indicators show a decline in productivity.

This year's *hikes* in the cost of living have made it even more difficult for those living on fixed incomes.

hinder—v.   obstruct; hamper

hindrance—n.   e: Distrust among trading partners has been the major *hindrance* in closing the deal.
The rapid increase in environmental-protection regulations is often seen as *hindering* the formation of new companies.

hindsight—n.   perception of events after their occurrence
e: We can see now, with the benefits of *hindsight,* that some countries adjusted quickly by increasing exports.
In the new president's acceptance speech, he stressed the importance of using *hindsight* to avoid the mistakes of the past.

hinge—v.   depend; be contingent upon
e: The success of the contract talks *hinges* mainly on whether management and the union are willing to compromise.
Her promotion *hinged* on how successful she was with the new client.
origin: hinge—metal fastener that connects a door to its frame

hitch—n.   impediment; delaying problem
e: The *hitch* in the agreement is whether Syria ultimately will follow the deal.
Negotiators have run into a *hitch* in their talks with the inmates; the prison remains under siege.
origin: hitch—knot

hoard—v.   hide; store

hoard—n.   e: An African spokesman accused developed countries of *hoarding* scientific and technological advances.
Police have discovered *hoards* of weapons in Tamil rebels' strongholds.

hobble—v.   1. hinder, restrain; 2. move slowly and awkwardly
e: This year's downturn in the world economy *hobbled* Africa.
The company has been *hobbling* along for the last twenty years, never showing great profit, but refusing to go bankrupt.

hogwash—n.   nonsense; worthless talk
e: People at all levels began to realize that the president's showy speech was all *hogwash.*
The representative referred to misdoings in his personal life as *hogwash.*
origin: hog—pig

hover—v.   be in state of uncertainty or suspense
e: A dark cloud has *hovered* over Washington recently as Congress continues to be unable to resolve budget problems.
The Dow Jones Industrial Average has *hovered* around the 2000 mark for a week.

hub—n.   center of activity or interest
e: The *hub* of the city has gradually moved southward as businesses move away from the slums to the north.
The Federal Reserve Board has become the *hub* of investors' attention as they set policy for the coming year.
origin: hub—center of a wheel

hurdle—v.   overcome; surmount

hurdle—n.   e: Gary Hart has a big *hurdle* to overcome if he hopes to make it to the White House.

The main question now is whether the U.S. economy can *hurdle* its trade deficits.

origin: hurdle—obstacle to be leapt over in a race

hurly-burly—n.   uproar; tumult

e: The *hurly-burly* on the floor of the stock exchange contributed to the drop in share prices.

Amid the *hurly-burly* following the gunshot, the killer managed to escape.

hush—v.   calm; quiet

hush—n.   e: He was put in prison for two years to *hush* him up.

A *hush* fell over the courtroom as the judge came out to deliver the sentence.

hustings—n.   local court; proceeding of elections

e: Her campaign manager thinks her preliminary media exposure is just as important as her appearance at the *hustings*.

Local officials are busy with political *hustings* this week in preparation for the upcoming election.

CHAPTER V

I–J–K WORDS

impair—v. diminish in strength; make worse
impairment—n. e: The chairman's judgment was *impaired* by a threatened management shake-up.
Investing in such unpredictable ventures will *impair* the financial health of the company.

impend—v. menace; be about to occur
impending—adj. e: A shortage of rail cars and *impending* financial problems have long plagued the national railway system.
The *impending* visit of Pope John Paul II to Spain has been long awaited by Spanish Catholics.

imperil—v. endanger
e: The new Soviet demands are seen as *imperiling* talks in Geneva.
Her personal quarrels with the vice-president have *imperiled* her blossoming career.

impoundment—n. act or state of collecting; confined
impound—v. e: The Soviet Union is believed to have invented the Eurodollar to discourage any U.S. attempt at *impoundment.*

incense—adj. cause passion or extreme anger
e: He was *incensed* by the press claims of his mismanagement and threatened to sue for slander.
Officials were *incensed* by the violation of Japanese airspace by Soviet military planes.

inception—n. commencement; origin; beginning
e: Since the *inception* of the plan two years ago, our progress has been remarkable.
The talks are still in the stage of *inception;* it is difficult to say if an agreement can be reached.

inch—v. move slowly, by small degrees
inch—n. e: Israeli forces *inched* another block into PLO-held West Beirut.
The president has *inched* his way from the far right to a more moderate stand.

incumbent—n.   official holding a specific office
incumbent—adj.
incumbency—n.   e: The polls heavily favor *incumbents* over challengers.
The *incumbent* announced that he would not seek reelection.

inexorable—adj.   relentless; inflexible
e: Time marches *inexorably* forward.
Such *inexorable* policies have drawn her criticism as being unwilling to take new circumstances into consideration.

instill—v.   introduce; implant gradually and deeply
instillment—n.   e: The rebels were accused of attempting to *instill* fear into the people.
From an early age Chinese children are *instilled* with a love for the motherland.

intercourse—n.   communication; contact
e: We have had peaceful *intercourse* concerning our mutual trade interests.
Since the civilian president took over, *intercourse* with other countries has increased steadily.

intertwine—v.   weave together
intertwinement—n.   e: The continent's economies have grown so *intertwined* that countries now depend greatly on each other's continuing prosperity.
India's economic and population problems are *intertwined*; progress on one would lead to progress on the other.
origin: twine—thread; string

inveigh—v.   strongly protest
e: The Polish leader *inveighed* against the strikes, saying they were harmful to everyone.
Students all over the world continue to *inveigh* against South Africa's apartheid policies.

irksome—adj.   tedious, bothersome
irk—v.   e: The Soviets found Kohl's talk of the ultimate goal of German unity particularly *irksome.*
The boss was *irked* by his employee's consistent lateness.

jagged—adj.   having a harsh, rough, irregular shape
e: Commerce takes place at four designated ports along the *jagged* coastline.
An old, *jagged* knife was found not far from the victim's body.

jacked up—adj.   raised
e: Since late 1973, when OPEC *jacked up* its charge for a barrel of oil, conservation measures have been implemented around the world.
Merchants took advantage of the country's food shortages to *jack up* prices to unbelievably high levels.
origin: jack—tool for raising a car

jangle—v.   grate on; jar
e: Their unconventional politics are *jangling* the nerves of the establishment here.
origin: jangle—harsh, metallic sound

jeopardy—n.   danger; exposure to death; loss or injury

jeopardize—v.   e: The tiny country is in *jeopardy* of being swallowed up by its neighbors.
By getting involved in smuggling, she *jeopardized* her entire career.

jettison—v.   discard; cast away

jetsam—n.   e: The Reagan administration decided to *jettison* human rights as the
cornerstone of U.S. foreign policy.
The bureau was seen as *jetsam* and removed from the budget.
origin: jettison—throw cargo out of a ship, aircraft, or spacecraft

jitters—n.   sense of panic or nervousness
jittery—v.
jittery—adj.   e: Inflation *jitters* seem to be affecting trading behavior.
His *jittery* behavior at conferences makes him a disaster at the bargaining table.

jockey—v.   maneuver for advantage
e: Reagan indicated he would not allow himself to be outmatched in the *jockeying* with
Gorbachev.
Banes is the most experienced of those *jockeying* for the chairmanship.
origin: jockey—professional horse rider

joust—v.   combat personally; engage in competition
joust—n.   e: The trial continued after some legal *jousting* between the defense and
lawyers for the civil plaintiffs.
The unsuccessful candidates are now *jousting* for media exposure to make themselves
attractive candidates for the vice-presidency.
origin: joust—fight between two knights on horses

kickback—n.   return of a percentage of a sum received by confidential agreement
e: *Kickbacks* and price-boosting by manufacturers of heart pacemakers may be costing
the U.S. $200 million a year.
Customs officials were convicted of accepting *kickbacks* from exports secretly allowed to
exceed quotas.

knuckle under—v.   yield to pressure
e: Schultz is hoping to reach an agreement without *knuckling under* to the Soviets.
The regional manager *knuckled under* from the years of intense negotiations and was
forced to retire early.
origin: knuckle—finger joint

CHAPTER VI

L–M WORDS

lackluster—adj.   dull; lacking interest
e: Stock prices were slightly higher today, extending a *lackluster* recovery from last week.
The government seems incapable of breathing any life into the *lackluster* economy.
origin: luster—brilliance; shininess

lair—n.   bed; den
e: Daniel descended into the lion's *lair*. The wolves had a *lair* up on the hillside.

lambaste—v.   attack verbally
e: He has decorated the walls of his office with originals of the cartoons that *lambasted* him during his ordeal.
Rebel leaders have gained support by *lambasting* the Reagan administration.

lame duck—n.   official holding office during the period between an election and the time the newly elected official takes office.
e: The report of the *lame-duck* commission came only a week before they were to give way to the new officials.
Reagan called the Senate back for a *lame-duck* session to finish necessary business before the new Congress was convened.
origin: lame duck—weakling

lapse—v.   decline; become invalid
lapse—n.   e: Prime Minister-elect Gonzales, a *lapsed* Catholic, is expected to meet the Pope when he comes to town on Thursday.
Bombing began again yesterday after a *lapse* of almost a week.

larceny—n.   theft; robbery
larcenous—adj.   e: The head accountant was arrested on a grand-*larceny* charge.
The man was charged with petty *larceny* for using stolen automobile license plates.

at large—adj.   1. freely moving;
2. not representing a specific group.
e: Police have reported that the killer is still *at large.*
Besides members of each of the city's various ethnic groups, some committee members were chosen from the community *at large.*

lash out—v.   make a strong verbal attack
e: President Menem is *lashing out* at the opposition amid rumours of a coup attempt.
The new president vowed to *lash out* at inflation and increase economic growth.

latch onto—v.   cling to; get hold of
e: Insiders say several high-ranking officials have *latched onto* some causes espoused by the Soviet leader.
Reagan has *latched onto* a policy of not raising taxes but is now forced to compromise.

lavish—v.   expend; squander
lavish—adj.
lavishness—n.   e: Candidates who blame the country's problems on *lavish* spending tend not to succeed so often.
People often overestimate his wealth because of his *lavish* and showy lifestyle.

leash—n.   restraint; limit
e: The Hondurans and U.S. officials can still tighten the *leash* on the rebels.
Reagan has not been able to keep his campaign promise to put a *leash* on spending.
origin: leash—restraining chain for an animal

level—v.   smooth; equalize; balance
e: The earthquake *leveled* many homes.
The army went about *leveling* the enemy city.

libel—n.   written statement unfairly harming another's reputation; defamation of character
libel—v.
libelous—adj.   e: The *libel* suit is based on the newspaper's allegedly false accusations about her private life.
It is very difficult for a public figure to prove *libel* in this country, making the press more bold about printing personal information.

linger—v.   persist, stay on
e: Clouds of protest *linger* as Waldheim attempts to stay in office despite questions of his Nazi involvement.
Lingering doubts about the president's leadership abilities have hurt him in recent polls.

lodge—v.   deliver or register (a complaint)
e: Papers formally requesting the extradition were *lodged* with the State Department.
Japan has *lodged* a protest against U.S. sanctions against the Toshiba Corporation.

loose end—n.   fragment of unfinished business
e: Only a few *loose ends* need to be tied up before the contract can be signed.
She stayed late in the office that night, tying up *loose ends* before her vacation.
"tie up loose ends"—finish remaining bits of work

lopsided—adj. not balanced, not symmetrical
lopsidedness—n. e: The Democrats swept the state of Maryland by *lopsided* margins.
The recovery ahead is predicted to be a *lopsided* one in which consumer spending
flourishes while industrial investment lags behind.

ludicrous—adj. ridiculous
ludicrousness—n. e: Although the minister dismisses accusations of his misdoings as
ludicrous, there is growing pressure for him to resign.
State Department officials have commented that the amateurish economic planning of
the Nicaraguan government is *ludicrous.*

lull—n. inactive period
lull—v. e: The treasury market faces a three-week *lull* in new note and bond financing.
The "War of the Cities" between Iran and Iraq resumed today after a *lull* of two weeks.

lurch—v. stagger; move unsteadily or abruptly
lurch—n. e: In recent years the economy has simply *lurched* from crisis to crisis, without
any sign of hope for stability.
The motorcade *lurched* to a halt as a bomb exploded in the front car.

lurk—v. sneak; wait in hiding
e: Financial collapse has been *lurking* for the mismanaged company.
Dubiel's past has been an issue *lurking* in the background throughout the campaign.

maddening—adj. enraging; deeply irritating
madden—v. e: The bureaucracy involved with getting even the simplest things done in
Russia can become *maddening.*
He gave up politics for a private law practice in order to get away from the *maddeningly*
fast pace.
origin: mad—insane, crazy

maim—v. cripple; incapacitate
e: Hundreds were killed and thousands were maimed during the bloody border
clashes.
Some Vietnam veterans have been *maimed*—not in body—but in spirit.

mar—v. damage; spoil
e: Relations between the firm's partners have improved greatly; the kind of disputes
that *marred* last year's meetings are not expected to recur.
Schmidt complained that lack of consultation has *marred* allied relations.

marshal—v. arrange in order
e: Their Government has now had more than two years to prepare their cases and *marshal* the necessary evidence.

meager—adj. thin; skimpy
meagerness—n. e: Teachers gathered near the White House yesterday to protest what
they see as *meager* spending increases for America's troubled education system.
The union's asking for two more days of paid holidays seems a *meager* request compared to their previous demands.

meddle—v.   interfere in what is not one's affair

meddler—n.   e: The government's charges of Soviets *meddling* in Afghanistan's internal affairs drew broad support across the political spectrum.

Presidential candidates have been complaining that the press is *meddling* in their private lives.

mend—v.   repair; improve

mend—n.   e: The index of leading indicators rose—a clear sign that the economy is on the *mend*.

The present peace talks among top leaders is the latest attempt to *mend* fences in Latin America.

mire—v.   stuck; unable to move or change

miry—adj.   e: The economy is *mired* in the deepest recession since World War II.

The stock market has been *mired* around the 2000 mark for weeks.

origin: mire—bog; deep, muddy area

misdemeanor—n.   less serious crime or offense

e: Although she is a known drug smuggler, she was only charged with possession of marijuana; a *misdemeanor*.

Shoplifting and other *misdemeanors* are on the rise in major French cities.

monopoly—n.   exclusive control; possession or command of supply

monopolist—n.

monopolization—n.

monopolize—v.

monopolist—adj.

monopolistic—adj.   e: Britain has lead the continent in privatizing several industries which formerly were run by state *monopoly*.

Regulation of the airplane industry is said to have *monopolized* the field by creating too many expenses for smaller firms.

mop up—v.   complete an action; finish the final details

e: The government forces are now in complete control of the islands; the last pocket of resistance was *mopped* up at daybreak.

Agreement has finally been reached on the Afghanistan treaty, leaving only a few details to be *mopped up* before the signing next week.

origin: mop—absorbent household tool used to clean floors.

motley—adj.   heterogeneous; varied

e: The celebration of the mayor's inauguration drew a *motley* crowd, with businessmen eating together with street workers.

The Department of Health, Education and Welfare was a *motley* collection of agencies doing totally unrelated work.

mount—v.   increase; set up

e: The general has set a date for elections amid *mounting* pressure for more democracy.

When Mexico ran short of cash, major nations *mounted* an immediate operation to refinance its debt.

muddle—v.　mix up; confuse; bungle

muddle—n.　e: Bankers hope to *muddle* through the world debt crisis without sustaining crippling losses.

The contradictory messages coming from the White House and the Federal Reserve Board have *muddled* investors, resulting in a directionless stock market.

muffle—v.　suppress; conceal

e: The White House hopes to *muffle* the protectionist lobby in order to keep European allies content.

Amnesty International has issued a report accusing the ruling party of *muffling* dissenting opinions.

origin: muffler—device to absorb sound

mug—v.　rob; beat

mugger—n.　e: The mayor of Tel Aviv and his wife were *mugged* on a New York City street.

The *mugger* was held by local residents until police arrived.

muggy—adj.　warm and humid

mugginess—n.　e: This summer's unusually *muggy* heat has caused construction projects to fall behind schedule.

The arguing at the conference has been aggravated by the *muggy*, tropical climate.

mug shot—n.　picture of a person in police records

e: *Mug shots* were taken of all the suspects gathered in the city's latest attempt to combat organized crime.

The rapist was picked out of a series of *mug shots* reviewed by his victim.

origin: mug—face; shot—picture

murky—adj.　obscure; gloomy; dark

murk—n.

murkiness—n.　e: Leading West German newspapers urged Stern to clarify the *murky* origins of the fake diaries.

The administration's nuclear war policy stance remains *murky* since officials have not made a definite statement on the "first strike" question.

muster—v.　gather up; assemble

e: A conference of factory representatives has been called in Cuba to *muster* support for an unpopular austerity program.

Local residents were unable to *muster* the courage to report the gang's activities to the police.

mute—v.　soften; subdue

e: The *muted* lights enhanced the elegance of the King's reception room

Bush's criticisms have been *muted* by his efforts to support the President.

origin: mute—person physically unable to speak

mutiny—n.　open rebellion, often of sailors or soldiers

mutinous—adj.

mutineer—n.

mutiny—v.　e: What appeared as imminent *mutiny* by the Salvadoran Air Force was averted today by an offer for a dialogue between the military and the government.

Mutinous troops stormed the palace and took over the radio and television stations.

mutter—v.   grumble; murmur
  e: *Mutters* filled the room as the President again denied being involved in the Iran-Contra affair.
  The delegation walked out of the U.N. session, *muttering* protests of the speaker's accusations.

muzzle—v.   prevent from speaking freely
muzzle—n. e: The *Post* accused various officials of trying to *muzzle* the press in Hong Kong.
  She has been effectively *muzzled* by anonymous phone calls threatening her family.
  origin: muzzle—device put over a dog's mouth to prevent it from biting

myriad—n.   a very large number
myriad—adj. e: Diplomatic staff is trained in a four year program in a *myriad* of fields.
  The modern financial markets offer a *myriad* of ways to invest money.

CHAPTER VII

N–O WORDS

nourish—v.   feed; maintain; support

nourishment—n. e: The rice-based diet of Southeast Asia has led to poor *nourishment* in several countries.

Over the years, the U.S. has sought to *nourish* good relations with islands in the Pacific.

nudge—v.   push gently in order to gain attention

nudge—n. e: West Germany is considering lowering interest rates to help *nudge* its economy toward faster growth.

Shultz's failure to *nudge* the Syrians toward troop withdrawals was expected as they had previously refused any compromise.

obliterate—v.   remove completely; destroy; wipe out

obliteration—n. e: Police failed to cordon off a large area at the murder site, causing the possible *obliteration* of vital evidence.

Border cities have been *obliterated* by the years of fighting between Iran and Iraq.

offspring—n.   young; children

e: Pandas generally give birth to only one *offspring*.

Robertson's claim of being the *offspring* of a U.S. Senator has won him more ridicule than admiration.

onslaught—n.   violent attack

e: The government was beginning to crack under the *onslaught* of various disclosures of its involvement in drug trade.

Banks have been hit with an *onslaught* of borrowers unable to repay their loans because of the recession.

outlandish—adj.   bizarre; strange

e: Kemp's call for a return to the gold standard is seen as *outlandish* by his rivals.

The princess's *outlandish* behavior in public has been a source of embarrassment for the royal family.

outrage—v. offend; cause to become angry
outrage—n.
outrageous—adj.
outrageousness—n. e: Arab nations have expressed their *outrage* at Israel's treatment of the Palestinians living in the West Bank.
The city council's decision to phase out rent control has *outraged* residents of the affected housing complexes.

outright—adj. entire; complete; thorough
outright—adv. e: Stockman's *outright* economic policy is the restoration of a balanced budget.
U.S. officials again have accused the Soviet Union of *outright* treaty violations.

outrun—v. escape; exceed
e: Palestinians who flee to Honduras fail to *outrun* violence.
The government has consistently allowed expenditures to *outrun* receipts, causing a huge budget deficit.
origin: "outdo"—exceed in performance

outsmart—v. get the better off; outwit
e: Canada, by *outsmarting* the government, may sharply reduce regulation of itself.
The FBI was simply *outsmarted* by the drug runners, resulting in millions of dollars worth of cocaine crossing the borders again last year.
origin: "outdo" exceed in performance

overman—v. have/get too many men for need
e: The government has trimmed payrolls in *overmanned* state firms.

override—v. dominate; declare null
e: Market stability is of *overriding* importance to developing nations.
Congress has voted to *override* the president's veto of legislation to introduce new import quotas.

overripe—adj. passed beyond ripeness or maturity
e: Capitalism has become *overripe* in some countries.
The grapes are *overripe.*

oversee—v. supervise; survey; examine
overseer—n. e: The defendant was *overseeing* the property while the owner was on vacation.
Williamson *oversees* the work of several parliamentary committees.

overt—adj. not hidden; open
e: It does no appear that *overtly* illegal actions took place in the casinos, but investigators are questioning suspects about a secret prostitution ring.
Overt aid to the dictator has been cut off, but insiders say funding is being continued through other sources.
opposite: covert

43

overture—n.   proposal; beginning

e: The President's critical speech gave a clear signal that no *overtures* to improve U.S.–Soviet relations will be coming soon.

The delegation's first visit served as an *overture* to the present trade agreements.

origin: overture—musical introduction to a longer work

overturn—v.   revoke a previous legal or legislative decision

e: Legislation that calls for *overturning* of job racial quotas was introduced today.

The conviction was *overturned* by the U.S. Court of Appeals.

CHAPTER VIII

P–Q–R WORDS

pall—n.   covering of gloom or foreboding
e: The banking collapse cast a *pall* over the economy.
Accusations of spying have thrown a *pall* over superpower relations.
origin: pall—cloth for covering a coffin

pandemonium—n.   wild uproar or noise
e: The gun battle in the street led to *pandemonium* as people tried to scatter.
Initial drops in the stock market index caused *pandemonium* on the exchange floor, which led to the crash in prices.

pang—n.   sharp, sudden feeling of pain or distress
e: Hart discussed the *pangs* of guilt he felt about his love affair.
She felt *pangs* of anxiety every time she had to speak in public.

pare—v.   remove; reduce
e: Spending on railway construction will be *pared* ten percent because of a declining number of users.
Federal agencies that duplicate work done at the local level need to be *pared* from the budget.
origin: pare—cut away the peel of

parson—n.   clergyman; rector
parsonage—n.   e: He is the *parson* of the old church.
Go fetch the *parson* please.

partisan—n.   strong supporter of one party or ideology
partisan—adj.
partisanship—n.   e: Her speech had a *partisan* tone, showing that she is still seeking to build her support base in the party.
He is an old *partisan* of the Yugoslavian army.

peddle—v.   sell; offer for sale

peddler—n.   e: False documents were *peddled* to tourists to gain much needed hard currency.

Newspaper *peddlers* have been warned to stay off the street at night because of the recent outbreak of urban violence.

peek—v.   watch secretly; glance quickly

peek—n.   e: This month's trade figures give us a *peek* at what the trade balance will look like this year.

When he was younger, he was arrested for *peeking* into his neighbors' windows.

peg—v.   stabilize

e: If interest rates alone are *pegged* while the value of the dollar is free to vary, the dollar could fall sharply.

The president has *pegged* the number of government workers to last month's level in an attempt to slow the growth of the federal government.

origin: peg—small, cylindrical fastener

peg out—v.   categorize; sort out

e: "Talk to your mum while I *peg out* my washing."

perfunctory—adj.   acting routinely; done with little care

e: The ambassador's wife's smile was an uncertain one; *perfunctory* and quick to fade.

A *perfunctory* ratification of the charter was completed today after only a short discussion.

perk—n.   fringe benefit associated with a position; perquisite

e: He has lost the support of the people for his cause due to his love of the *perks* of exile politics.

Labor costs are even higher because of higher wages, longer holidays and other *perks* needed to attract workers.

persuade—v.   convince; move by argument
persuasion—n.
persuasive—adj.   e: The salesman *persuaded* me to try the new product.

The lawyer tried to *persuade* the jury with her arguments.

pervade—v.   become diffused; spread throughout

pervasive—adj.   e: No one really knows if there is more stress now than in the past, but many experts believe it has become *pervasive*.

Although work continues as usual, a feeling of tension *pervades* the embassy after a bomb was discovered in the bathroom yesterday.

phony—adj.   fake; fictitious; spurious
phony—n.
phoniness—adj.   e: She was convicted of trying to sell over a million dollars of *phony* loans.

The *phoniness* of his character has kept his campaign from gaining much support.

pique—n.   resentment caused by injured pride

pique—v.   e: Officials of Opus Del attribute the attacks to *pique* and personal problems.

She was *piqued* about not being invited to speak at the convention.

plaintiff—n.   party that files a suit in a law case
e:. The *plaintiff* and the defense appeared before the judge today in a preliminary hearing.
The City of New York is the *plaintiff* in the pollution trial.
origin: plaint—complaint

pledge—n.   formal promise; oath
pledge—v.   e: The conference offers a *pledge* to increase aid for blacks from poor neighborhoods.
Reagan *pledged* to cut the federal deficit in his 1980 election campaign.

plight—n.   difficult or poor condition
e: The city has stepped up measures to ease the *plight* of the homeless.
Nothing arouses more pity than the *plight* of children in the middle of war zones.

plum—n.   something desirable
e: Chile's Pinochet has offered political *plums* to key officials in an effort to keep unrest from spreading.
The position of envoy to the U.N. is a *plum* which might just satisfy Jackson.
origin: plum—purplish, fleshy fruit

plummet—v.   fall sharply; plunge
e: The country is in need of a solid plan to prop *plummeting* commodity prices.
The Dow Jones Average *plummeted* over a hundred points as the figures on the trade balance were worse than expected.
origin: plumb—weight used to show an exact vertical

plunder—v.   pillage; steal; sack
plunder—n.
plunderer—n.   e: Marxists see the flourishing of capitalist economies as the result of *plundering* abroad.
Guerrillas have *plundered* villages in the south, raising doubts as to the strength of the ruling military commander.

pogrom—n.   massacre of a minority group
e: Tsarist Russia had a long tradition of *pogroms* against Jews.
Chinese officials stated that it was ridiculous to claim that any sort of *pogrom* had occurred in Tibet.

pokey—n.   jail
e: Somehow, Nixon managed to establish the idea that if a public figure can stay out of the *pokey*, everything else is okay.

pound—v.   strike repeatedly; beat heavily
e: The better-equipped loyalist troops *pounded* the advancing attackers.
The border town was *pounded* by short range missiles from Iraq.

premise—n.   idea which acts as the basis for an argument
premise—v.   e: The other candidates attacked Stone's *premise* that spending on welfare had been seriously cut in the past two years.
He *premised* his remarks with a review of the evidence.

probe—v.   examine closely; investigate
probe—n.   e: Already, three detectives involved in *probing* the millionaire's financial activities have been killed.
Another *probe* has been sent up in space to provide more detailed information about the other planets in our solar system.

proceeds—n.   profits
e: The *proceeds* of the concert will be donated to AIDS research centers.
The partners agreed to evenly split the *proceeds* of their overseas ventures.

prod—v.   urge; encourage
prod—n.   e: She has persisted in her non-nuclear stance despite *proddings* by the U.S.
Falling prices have *prodded* consumers to increase spending on household appliances.

proxy—n.   person authorized to act for another
e: The by-laws of the company's charter allow for voting by *proxy* if the board member is not present.
She agreed to act as his *proxy* at meetings during the time he was out of the country.

pummel—v.   pound; beat
pommel (var. of *pummel*)—v.   e: Gunboats off the coast joined in the *pummeling* of the enemy vessel.
His body was found *pommeled* in an alley; probably the work of angry debt collectors.

punctuate—v.   interrupted periodically
e: The calm was occasionally *punctuated* by the sounds of carefree children laughing.
Her captors then began a twenty-four hour drive, *punctuated* only by stops for gasoline.
origin: punctuation—marks used in writing to separate units.

purport—v.   profess; claim
e: Having examined the *purported* Hitler diaries, government experts concluded that they were clearly forged.
The conference on Latin American tensions did not *purport* to provide a definitive set of solutions, only to clarify opposing viewpoints.

pursuant to—adj.   in agreement with; in accord with
e: *Pursuant to* orders, the police placed the minister under house arrest.
Missile reductions have taken place *pursuant to* the treaty signed last year.

pursuit—n.   occupation; act of pursuing
e: I was delayed with his *pursuit* of information.
The *pursuit* of happiness is the ultimate goal.

quarry—n.   1. game for hunting;
2. source of minerals
e: Ranchers have requested that the wolf, growing steadily in number, be once again considered legal *quarry*.
The *quarries* of Vermont are a source of marble for all of New England.

quash—v.   suppress completely
e: The hijackers have refused to compromise their demands, a development that *quashed* hopes for any immediate action.
Government forces easily *quashed* the rebellion that started in the southwest jungles.

quibble—v.   raise unimportant objections; argue pettily
quibble—n.
quibbler—n.   e: *Quibbling* still threatens the unity of the ATM Network.
Cabinet members have been constantly *quibbling* among themselves, which makes experts question the president's leadership abilities.

quirk—n.   peculiar; strange
quirkiness—n.
quirky—adj.   e: Albania's *quirky* defiance of the rest of the world has resulted in an increasingly backward economy.
The minister's insistence on early morning negotiations is just a personal *quirk*.

racket—n.   illegal enterprise
racketeer—n.   e: Four members of the Bouano crime family were convicted for a *racketeering* conspiracy.
Miami police have had little luck fighting against the city's numerous drug *rackets*.

rally—v.   1. recover;
2. mass meeting to foster enthusiasm for a cause
rally—n.   e: The credit market *rallied* after the release of March's favorable trade balance.
Stocks closed higher in Tokyo yesterday following a *rally* in New York.
A *rally* was held in Washington to gather support for the Equal Rights Amendment.
Jackson's energizing speeches at his campaign *rallies* have drawn support for him from many sectors of society.

rampage—n.   course of violent behavior
rampage—v.   e: The city has been terrorized by a *rampage* of killings which has even extended to babies.
Rioters protesting an increase in transport fares went on a *rampage*, causing extensive damage to two buses.

rampant—adj.   unrestrained; unchecked
e: Inflation, which has long been *rampant* in the little country, began to spread to its neighbors.
AIDS has been running *rampant* throughout the gay communities of major U.S. cities.

ransack—v.   plunder; pillage
ransacker—n.   e: The thieves *ransacked* the residence, making off with jewelry and cash estimated to be worth twenty thousand pounds.
Guerrillas *ransacked* the village to try to maintain supplies for their troops.

rap—v.   reprimand; criticize
rap—n.   e: A senior aide *rapped* the president's economic policy, claiming it ignored the growing debt crisis.
Hungary *rapped* Israel for action taken at its embassy last week.
origin: rap—strike quickly

rapport—n.   relationship of mutual trust
   e: A Japanese spokesman, responding to a question on U.S.–Japan relations, stated "Our *rapport* with the Americans has not changed."
   The Iran–Contra affair was supposedly an attempt to establish *rapport* with moderate Iranian leaders.

rapprochement—n.   commencement of or maintaining a cordial relationship
   e: The *rapprochement* between the Soviets and the Iranians makes the Kuwaiti government nervous.
   This has been a decade of *rapprochement* in several areas of the world.

reap—v.   obtain; receive; win
   e: Japan is now *reaping* the rewards of careful economic planning.
   Several companies have *reaped* huge profits from selective investment in Third World countries.
   origin: reap—harvest

rebound—v.   recover
rebound—n.   e: After seemingly losing support, the governing party has *rebounded* in a key state vote.
   Stock markets around the world *rebounded* today after yesterday's sharp drops.

rebuff—n.   abrupt refusal
rebuff—v.   e: The Soviets have received only a rude *rebuff* to their request for increasing technological cooperation.
   Israel *rebuffed* Reagan on his pullback requests, insisting they could handle their own affairs.

rebut—v.   refute by offering evidence
rebuttal—n.   e: A defector is helping U.S. officials to find and *rebut* Soviet disinformation.
   The president's speech will be followed by a *rebuttal* from the opposition party leader.

recant—v.   make a retraction of a previous statement
recantation—n.   e: She *recanted* her previous claims, publicly apologizing for being misled by incomplete information.
   A foreign ministry spokesman refused to *recant* his accusations of U.S. interference, despite evidence to the contrary.

recede—v.   decrease; retract; retreat
   e: U.S. influence over the internal affairs of other countries has been *receding* in recent years.
   The unrest that followed the election is *receding* as opposition leaders are beginning to look for ways to cooperate with the ruling party.

reckless—adj.   careless; uncontrolled
   e: Economists are blaming the recession on *reckless* government spending over the past several years.
   Simmons was arrested last night for *reckless* driving.

redemption—n.   act; fulfillment of repairing; paying
   e: Mutual funds suffered heavy net *redemptions*.

reel—v.   turn or move around; stagger
e: France was still *reeling* from the shock of the massacre when the terrorists struck again.
The mayoral candidate *reeled* around just as his assassin fired the gun.

rehash—n.   repeat
rehash—v.   e: Reporters were disappointed to find that the speech was just a *rehash* of existing policy
She refuses to *rehash* the story of her affair for the press.

relapse—v.   fall back after partial recovery, regress
relapse—n.   e: In the late 1940's, Europe was starving and Americans still feared a *relapse* of the Great Depression.
The aging writer suffered a *relapse* and had to be readmitted to the hospital.

relay—v.   pass from one group to another
e: The Soviet proposal was *relayed* by ministers to the U.S. State department.
Soldiers from the front *relayed* stories of chemical weapons being used on border towns.

relent—v.   soften; yield
relentless—adj.
relentlessness—n.   e: He *relented* to advocates of the plan on condition of his overseeing the initial stages.
The man who killed at least four black children is finally in jail due to *relentless* pursuit by the police.

relinquish—v.   release; give up; resign
relinquishment—n.   e: The Bolivian president must *relinquish* his power at the end of this term.
The chairman had *relinquished* authority for making such decisions to his assistants.

relish—v.   enjoy; get pleasure from
relishable—adj.
relish—n.   e: She *relished* a few moments by herself between negotiations.
Sorenson *relished* his victory after a three-day battle on the Senate floor.
origin: relish—condiment to add flavor to a meal

renege—v.   fail to carry out a commitment
e: Management accused the investors of *reneging* their funding commitments.
The local leader has often been accused of *reneging* his campaign promises.

repeal—v.   annul; revoke
e: Extremists advocate *repealing* all laws prohibiting the use and sale of drugs.
The court voted to *repeal* the controversial civil rights ruling.

reprieve—n.   delay of punishment
reprieve—v.   e: The former diplomat won a *reprieve* on Friday from grand jury testimony as to his role in the sale of arms to Iran.
She was granted a *reprieve* from her jail sentence in order to take care of family matters.

reprisal—n.   retaliation

e: The Israelis bombed cities in Lebanon in *reprisal* for attacks on the settlements.
The terrorists have threatened *reprisals* for the capture of their leader.

reshuffle—v.   reorganize

e: The day's schedule was *reshuffled* at the last minute because of a flight delay.
The president *reshuffled* his cabinet ministers after the Minister of Defense stepped down.

resolve—v.   decide firmly
resolution—n.
resolute—adj.   e: At her retirement, she was praised for her *resolve* in fighting corruption in the young country's leadership.
So far, Noriega has been *resolute* in his refusal to give in to U.S. demands.

respite—n.   temporarily put off; delay

e: The Mayor of Lyon said he wanted a *respite* from public life so he could spend more time with his family.
Shultz's meeting with Castro continued after a brief *respite* for lunch.

retrench—v.   cut down; reduced
retrenchment—n.   e: After his defeat in Congress, the president is *retrenching* his allies.
Chile's Pinochet *retrenches* in military power.
origin: trench—long, narrow hole used in warfare

revamp—v.   reconstruct; restore

e: Prime Minister Thatcher is expected to resist suggestions to *revamp* the voting system.
The company has *revamped* its product line, putting more emphasis on high-tech equipment.

rift—n.   break in friendly relations

e: Liberals are trying desperately to mend a dangerous party *rift*.
The efforts to impede the Trans-Siberian pipeline caused a serious *rift* between the U.S. and its allies.

rip–off—n.   theft; act of cheating

e: Some *rip–offs* thrive as others fade.
This store is a *rip–off*.
He really became a *rip–off*.

ripple—v.   spread throughout; permeate
ripple—n.
ripple—adj.   e: The theory asserts that gains for big business will *ripple* throughout the entire country.
The enthusiasm of the demonstration leaders had a *ripple* effect on the gathered people, who were soon chanting and screaming anti-government slogans.
origin: ripple—a small wave

rouse—v.   excite; awaken

e: The Congresswoman was given a *rousing* ovation as she entered the hall.
Jackson delivered yet another *rousing* speech, adding momentum to his growing popularity.

runoff—n.   extra competition to break a tie

e: The former Governor of Alabama was forced into a *runoff* yesterday as no candidate held a clear majority.

The constitution makes no provisions for *runoff* elections, allowing Roh to take office despite his lack of support.

CHAPTER IX

S–T WORDS

scam—n.   deceptive act or operation
e: Police say that such *scams* are out of control in the city.
She was previously arrested as part of a *scam* to defraud a local bar owner.

scanty—adj.   meager; barely enough
scant—adj.
scant—v. e: Funding for a power plant in Utah was discussed in a *scantily* attended joint session of the congress.
Unfortunately, there is *scant* evidence as to who was actually responsible for the security breakdown.

scapegoat—n.   one that bears blame for others
e: The U.S. is using the paramilitary leader as a *scapegoat* in the Salvadoran crisis.
It seems the more neutral a politician is, the easier it is for him to become a *scapegoat* for others.

scoff—v.   mock; address with derision
scoff—n. e: Reagan *scoffed* at reports that he has used astrology to determine his schedule.
Noriega's *scoffs* at U.S. threats show that he will attempt to remain in power.

score—n.   group of twenty
e: *Scores* of Palestinians were killed in Beirut in yesterday's fighting.
Survivors say they counted *scores* of corpses lying in the street.

score—v.   succeed; win
e: Supply-side extremists scored today in Congress with the passage of a budget containing many of their proposals.
Bush *scored* big on Super Tuesday, which should win him the Republican nomination.

scourge—n.   cause of affliction
scourge—v.   e: Economists used to believe that we would have to choose between the twin *scourges* of unemployment and inflation.
Meese has been nothing but a *scourge* for the Reagan administration.
origin: scourge—whip

scramble—v.   confuse; mix; move hurriedly
scramble—n.   e: His departure from the White House *scrambled* prospects for the 1988 presidential race.
Prices drop and OPEC *scrambles* to keep them from going into a free fall.

scuffle—n.   disorderly struggle
scuffle—v.   e: Police contend that upon hearing the *scuffle*, they entered the home to break it up.
Stern's *scuffle* with reporters last year remains an embarrassment to his campaign.

scuttle—v.   ruin; destroy
e: A plan to decrease subsidies to farming was *scuttled* by a strong lobby movement.
A shortage of money available for mortgages may *scuttle* the industry's modest recovery.
origin: scuttle—sink a ship

secession—n.   withdrawal, usually of one part of a country from the rest
secede—v.   e: The Dalai Lama's call for Tibetan *secession* was strongly criticized by a Chinese government spokesman.
Aquino made it clear that no part of the Philippines would be allowed to *secede* under her administration.

seesaw—v.   alternate up and down
seesaw—adj.   e: Interest rates have been *seesawing* for the past few months, sending mixed signals to investors.
The president's popularity *seesawed* during her first year, but gradually she has gained the people's support.
origin: seesaw—a board balanced in the middle used as a playground toy

seethe—v.   be agitated
e: A *seething* dispute has grown between the Polish government and striking workers.
The head of the Hong Kong Exchange *seethed* in anger at the accusation that he had acted illegally.

seize—v.   grab suddenly; take possession legally
seizure—n.   e: Arms reportedly headed for the IRA were *seized* by French officials last week.
The judge ordered the *seizure* of the defendant's property if payment of the fine could not be made.

severance—n.   extra pay given an employee upon leaving
e: Almost 40 percent of the staff was laid off and given two week's *severance* pay.
The African region remained unscathed, but only because all workers had *severance* clauses in their contracts.
origin: sever—cut; divide

shed—v.   give, set off or out
e: In hot weather, dogs *shed* their fur.
The boys *shed* their clothes by the banks of the swimming hole.
The lady *shed* a tear.

shelve—v.   postpone; remove from service
e: A U.S. proposal for an IMF crisis fund is being *shelved* for now.
The old aircraft were *shelved* after the deployment of the army's new purchase.

shove—v.   push rudely
e: While Parrish was behind bars, two inmates grabbed him and *shoved* him into a cell.
People were pushing and *shoving* everywhere.

showdown—n.   event that forces an issue to a conclusion
e: A *showdown* between Arabs and the U.S. was put off today by an agreement to meet again next week on peace talks.
Stone-throwing by the mob forced a *showdown* with police that left two rioters dead.

shrapnel—n.   bits of artillery shell
e: The general was wounded by *shrapnel* when his motorcade was attacked by guerrilla forces.
Doctors removed *shrapnel* from near the heart of a villager caught in the crossfire.

shred—n.   small piece; scrap
shred—v.   e: There was not a *shred* of evidence to support that position.
The dog ripped the carpet to *shreds*.

shuffle—v.   mix in a disorderly way
shuffle—n.   e: By *shuffling* the cash, the military meet his payroll.
The attorney general has approved an unprecedented *shuffling* of funds to make up for the deficit.

shunt—v.   shift; move aside
shunt—n.   e: The railcar was *shunted* onto a sideway.
In his rush to the top of the corporate ladder, he *shunted* aside all his friends.
origin: shunt—move a train to another track

siding—v.   taking of sides/material; partisanship
siding—n.   e: Aluminum-*siding* buyers should be cautioned.
Siding can make your home better-looking and easier to care for.
I am *siding* with you.

sketchy—adj.   incomplete; superficial
e: Medical research is still *sketchy*.

slander—v.   utter a false or defamatory statement against someone.
slander—n.   e: She liked to spread vicious *slander* about people.
His family name was *slandered* by the television news, resulting in a lawsuit.

slap—n. rebuff an insult

e: The president took frequent pointed *slaps* at the rival union.

The administration *slapped* tough trade restrictions on all imports of specialty steel products.

slate—v. designate; schedule

e: A handicapped employee had been *slated* to lose his job.

The wide *slate* of new public offerings is good for the economy.

slavish—adj. oppressive

e: He *slavishly* imitates others.

He lavished *slavish* praise on her.

slick—adj. clever

e: There was *slick* maneuvering by the Senate.

slippage—n. unfinished or unnoticed pass

e: Given the present volatility of the electorate, any significant *slippages* during the campaign could result in fraud.

sloppy—adj. careless

e: In an apparent effort to prod an often sleepy and *sloppy* work force, management has become more strict.

slovenly—adj. untidy

e: Politicians attract votes during a period of recession by claiming that the party in power has a *slovenly* appearance.

He has a *slovenly* appearance.

slug—v. strike hard

e: Candidates were *slugging* it out in the Republican primary.

They *slugged* him in the stomach and beat him on the face.

sluggish—adj. slow in movement, growth, or flow

e: The river is very *sluggish* in summer.

The stock market was *sluggish* today.

He moved in a *sluggish* manner.

slung over—adj. thrown over

e: The police patrolling the streets may wear machine guns *slung over* their backs.

They lounge in the central square with automatic weapons carelessly *slung over* their laps.

slur—n. pass over

e: Mr. Nakasone had intended no *slur*.

The only reference to the Carter years is a calculated *slur*.

snap—v. give way abruptly

e: Gold bullion snapped back above four hundred U.S. dollars an ounce after its sharp decline.

snarl—v.   speak angrily; tangle
  e: . . . and their bureaucracy is split into two *snarling* fronts.

snarl—n.   a tangled situation
  e: The nation's bankruptcy-court system was imperiled by a legal *snarl.*

snipe—v.   shoot at enemy from cover
sniper—n.   e: There are reports of sporadic exchanges of gunfire between the army and
  PLO *snipers.*

snoop—v.   look furtively; pry
  e: *Snooping* around, he discovered the machine guns were not loaded.

snort—v.   inhale noisily
  e: The man would *snort* as much as seven grams of cocaine a day.

snub—v.   treat with scorn
  e: The Soviets *snub* the west's rights plan in Madrid.
  The controversy over Mrs. King's *snubbing* of Mr. Botha continues.

snugly—adj.   compact
  e: He assembled the bolt in the car *snugly.*
  We are *snugly* in our sleeping bags.

soberly—adj.   without exaggeration
  e: *Soberly,* these economists said there is no prospect of an automatic recovery.

spate—n.   sudden flow or wave
  e: A Soviet citizen, whose disappearance triggered a *spate* of rumors of spying, has requested asylum.
  There was a *spate* of requests to see the minister.

spawn—v.   bring forth
  e: Services themselves *spawn* technological advances.
  The steam engine helped *spawn* the Industrial Revolution.

spell—n.   short period of time
  e: The stock market closed at its second highest level in history today, bouncing back
  from a *spell* of profit-taking.

spoil—n.   prize; plunder; loot
  e: He is a fellow who believes in sharing the *spoils* with his family.
  The men quarreled over the division of the *spoils.*

spoof—n.   light parody
  e: Not even a sacred cow is free of this, as this *spoof* makes clear.
  The comedian made a big *spoof* of the president.

spotty—adj.   lacking consistency
  e: Response for a call for an eight-hour nationwide strike was *spotty.*

sprawl—v.   spread out awkwardly
e: They were dominated since Spanish colonial times by the white aristocratic minority centered in the *sprawling* capital of Lima.

spree—n.   lively activity
e: The stock market went on its biggest trading *spree* ever today.
A prison guard went on a shooting *spree* today, killing thirteen people.

sprout up—v.   begin to grow
e: Family businesses are *sprouting up* all over the place.

spur—v.   stimulate; set in action
e: He was *spurred* on by his success to ever-greater challenges.
She *spurred* the horse onward.

spurn—v.   reject
e: Both men said they *spurned* the material because of doubts about authenticity.
King Hussein is *spurning* an invitation from President Reagan to Washington.
Israeli authorities have *spurned* their appeals for recognition.

spurt—n.   jet; moment
e: With a *spurt* of energy she climbed up the stairs.
The horses *spurted* out of the starting gate.

squabble—v.   quarrel
e: There is not the least *squabbling* among producers over individual shares of the annual global quota.
Talks would end one of the alliance's more divisive *squabbles*.
The British Labor Party is beset by a *squabbler* despite a uniting quest.

squander—v.   spend wastefully
e: Stalin could subdue them, but why *squander* Russian energies keeping them down?
Foreign aid has been *squandered* on unprofitable industrial investments.

square—v.   settle; adjust
e: They focused most of their activities on *squaring* their position.
Anglicans *square* off on women.
The matter is *squared* in your area of expertise.

squelch—v.   suppress completely
e: Reagan moved last week to squelch rumors about Volcker's departure.
The White House and Justice Department are attempting to *squelch* a major internal dispute.

stagger—v.   shake; hesitate
e: *Staggering* under the weight of the piano, the movers collapsed on the ground.
He drank too much and *staggered* wildly about the street.

stalemate—n.   deadlock, specifically a position in chess
e: They see a military *stalemate* that at the least can be kept from getting worse.

stalk—v.   search or walk for prey
e: The lions were *stalking* their prey.
The FBI was *stalking* the suspected spy throughout the city.

stark—adj.   bare; blunt; severe
e: The *stark* position of this question left everyone annoyed.

startle—v.   cause a quick movement, as in fright
e: The reasons for his *startling* set of circumstances are several.
Don't *startle* me with more unsettling news.

stash—v.   store in a secret place
e: A judge had acquitted them of charges of treason and *stashing* weapons for use against the government.

staunch—adj.   firm; strong
e: The government has been *staunch* in its support of Washington's stand in the Geneva talks.
On the first trading day in March, silver stood *staunchly* at seventy U.S. dollars for the spot month of comex.

stave off—v.   keep off
e: Officials of the company are getting emergency cash to *stave off* bankruptcy.
The Lebanese president is fighting to *stave off* the potentially crippling fragmentation of his power base.

stem the flow—v.   stop; hold back
e: Bonn wanted to *stem the flow* of third-world refugees.

stifle—v.   suffocate; hold back
e: It has *stifled* the private sector and independent trade unions.
The worst slump in fifty years *stifles* global economy.

stint—n.   limitation in period of time
e: Kohl's short *stint* in power so far has boosted his popularity.

stopgap—n.   makeshift; resource
e: The president claimed that *stopgap* funding for government is bad for an economic situation.
Stopgap measures are short-term.

straddle—v.   stand, sit, or walk with legs apart
e: She *straddled* herself between the chairs.
Many potential voters *straddle* both sides of an issue in an election year.

strafe—v.   attack
e: Gunships *strafed* an area outside Beirut.

stranglehold—n.   illegal form or hold
e: Authorities attempted to break the *stranglehold* of the rangers.

strenuous—adj.   energetic; vigorous
e: The player made a *strenuous* effort.
Strenuous efforts cannot save the team.

stricture—n.   Something that limits or restricts; censure
e: He tempered such remarks with harsh *strictures* about the Soviet Union's arms build-up.
He was demonstrating the power of a regime unconstrained by the common *strictures* of morality.

strife—n.   discord; struggle; violent conflict
e: It is a development that seems likely to provoke even more *strife* between Hebron's Jewish settlers and Arab inhabitants.
For nearly two months, Tripoli has been the scene of intermittent but worsening *strife*.

stripped of—adj.   taken off; removed
e: An officer has been arrested and *stripped of* rank.

strumming—v.   play idly
e: For hours the crowd had been singing, *strumming* guitars, and clapping hands.

strut—v.   walk with pompous bearing
e: Young men *strut* the main square.

stutter—v.   hesitate; speak with hesitation
e: They grow at a weak and *stuttering* rate.

subdued—adj.   brought under control
e: The *subdued* demand for new credit continues to drive down cost.

subpoena—n.   legal writ requiring appearances in court
e: He was served with a *subpoena*.
The district attorney *subpoenaed* the defendant.

subside—v.   settle; descent
e: After the applause *subsided*, the president cracked, "I thought you were reading the papers."

subtle—adj.   delicate; obscure; crafty
e: He was a very *subtle* person.
She kept giving *subtle* hints that she was available for a date.

sully—adj.   taint; to mar the luster
e: Military justice starts legal proceedings against the exiled former interior minister for *sullying* the honor of the armed forces.

sundry—adj.   various; miscellaneous
e: There are various and *sundry* items here.
He made *sundry* comments.

surmount—v.   surpass; excel; overcome
  e: He imposed sharp limits on the resources, political strength, and common purposes need to *surmount* disputes.
  It is a *surmountable* task.
  The boys *surmounted* the bill.

swagger—v.   walk with insolent air
  e: The most infamous of them all was Mariano Melgarejo, a murderous, *swaggering* tyrant.

swap—n.   informal exchange
swap—v.   e: "Irangate" is a misguided *swap*.

swarm—v.   move or congregate in great numbers
swarm—n.   e: The demonstrators *swarmed* onto the church steps, booing loudly and chanting.

sway—v.   dominate; affect; influence
  e: Peruvian guerrillas *swayed* the government. That did not necessitate any changes in the leadership that has held *sway* for fifteen years.
  Europe has come increasingly under the *sway* of socialists.

swindler—n.   a person who cheats or defrauds
  e: We will fully clear the matter we have; there is no reason to protect the *swindler*.

swing—n.   act or movement to swing or drive power
  e: Saudi Arabia should act temporarily as a *swing* producer to bring output back.

swoop—v.   pounce swiftly; make a sudden attack
  e: Six bombers *swooped* from west of Sidon to attack.

tamper—v.   engage in underhanded dealings
  e: He faces felony charges on theft by deception, *tampering* with public records.

tantalize—v.   keeping a desired object out of reach
  e: The notion of Soviet involvement remains a *tantalizing* conjecture.

tantamount—adj.   equivalent in value or effect
  e: His actions were *tantamount* to treason.
  She was *tantamount* to his mind.

tantrum—n.   fit of bad temper
  e: Mother Nature threw a *tantrum* over the past, dumping snow on the sun lovers.

taut—adj.   tight; tense
  e: He held the rope *taut*.
  The sail was pulled *taut*.

teeter—v.   totter; seesaw
  e: Overburdened with debt, Latin American countries are *teetering* on default.

tenet—n. principle; dogma
    e: They voted for the major *tenets* of the economic program.

tepid—adj. lacking in passion or force
    e: He was interrupted twenty-six times by applause, though much of it seemed *tepid*.

thaw—v. melt; become mobile or active
    e: Frozen food must be *thawed* before cooking.
    The spring *thaw* came early this year.

thrifty—adj. prosperous; sparing
thrift—n. e: He is a *thrifty* person.
    Many products can be bought cheaply at a *thrift* store.

thunderous—adj. thunderlike; loud and booming
    e: His speeches were greeted with *thunderous* applause.
    The band received a *thunderous* ovation.

thwart—v. contravene; frustrate; torture
    e: Her plans were always *thwarted* in advance.
    The bank robbers were *thwarted* in their getaway attempt.

tiding—n. information; news
    e: The new year brings some bad *tidings* for just about everyone.

toddle—v. walk as a small child; stumble
toddler—n. e: "It's a very tense situation," said a mother of a teenager and a *toddler*.

torpor—n. lethargy; apathy
    e: Andropov has persistently worked to shake up the *torpor* that afflicts Soviet institutions.

toss—v. throw lightly
    e: They started *tossing* money out of a car.

tout—v. spy; give a tip; stick out
    e: A study *touts* looser fiscal policy.
    He *touted* his ideas in public.
    The Dow Industrial average features the most widely *touted* indicators.

trickle—v. proceed slowly; fall
    e: Trade only *trickles* today.

trifle—n. toy; idle thing
    e: Don't bother him with such *trifles*.
    It was a *trifling* matter.

tug—n. strong pull
    e: After a six-week *tug*-of-war, the clerk has agreed to pay back his taxes.
    As she complained about the heat, she *tugged* at her heavy flak jacket.

tumble—n.   roll out in confusion
   e: The stock market took a *tumble* today in selling.
   Experts have been hotly debating the impact of the *tumble*.

turf—n.   territory; piece of peat
   e: A *turf* fight between two house panels delays the highway trust-fund extension.

tussle—n.   fight; scuffle
   e: It was the latest round in a month-long *tussle*.

CHAPTER X

U–V–W–X–Y–Z WORDS

unabashed—adj.   not embarrassed
> e: It is an *unabashed* attempt to convince consumers to stop buying from any company doing business in South Africa.
> His *unabashed* attempt to take advantage of his brother's presidency has hurt the administration's credibility.

unbeknownst—adj.   unknown
> e: *Unbeknownst* to the KGB, she had already become a CIA double agent.
> It seems Colonel North had supposedly, *unbeknownst* to Reagan, arranged for funds to be transferred to the Nicaraguan rebels.

unblushing—adj.   shameless; unabashed
> e: She made *unblushing* remarks concerning her experience with the former television preacher.
> He *unblushingly* described his poverty-filled childhood.
> origin: blush—become red with embarrassment

uncanny—adj.   mysterious; strange
> e: The way she always appears at the right moment is really *uncanny*.
> He is well-known for his *uncanny* ability to win the president's approval on most major decisions.

undaunted—adj.   resolute; not discouraged
> e: *Undaunted* by the law, thousands of protesters took to the streets.
> Contras remain *undaunted* amid building threats from the Sandinista government to launch an assault to finish the country's civil war.

underdog—n.   expected loser
> e: As an *underdog* candidate, she has had to confront her opponent directly on the issues in order to get more attention.
> Bush campaign workers say he would welcome an *underdog* position coming out of the July conventions.

undergird—v.   support from beneath; sustain

e: The ideas that *undergird* the party's authority have lost their hold on the mass' imagination.

A policy of peaceful coexistence with the country's neighbors will *undergird* her campaign.

origin: girder—a supporting beam used in construction

underscore—v.   underline; emphasize

e: Navy leaders contend that the Falklands conflict *underscored* the need to increase deployment of Britain's ships around the world.

Last week's meeting *underscored* the gulf states' fundamental differences on what direction the alliance should be taking.

unfurl—v.   unroll; disclose

e: The blue-and-white flag was *unfurled* over the palace.

The prime minister has *unfurled* a new package of reforms to be presented to Parliament.

unleash—adj.   free from; let loose

e: The West German economic minister *unleashed* a public attack on recent government policy.

Police *unleashed* the dogs on the prisoners, saying they were afraid of a riot breaking out.

origin: leash—restraining chain for a dog

unrelenting—adj.   constant; not diminishing in intensity

e: The president has always been an *unrelenting* advocate of free trade.

The regime's *unrelenting* persecution of political prisoners has drawn it criticism from all sides.

unruffled—adj.   calm; not upset

e: Japan is *unruffled* by textile cuts and continues to promote other, more successful exports.

Schmidt is *unruffled* by internal resistance to planned increases in military spending.

unscathed—adj.   not injured; unharmed

e: Mr. Ghandi escaped *unscathed* from the shooting.

All cabinet ministers have emerged from the investigation *unscathed.*

uphold—v.   affirm; support

e: The Supreme Court unanimously *upheld* the constitutionality of the windfall profit tax.

The president vowed to *uphold* the newly approved constitution.

uproot—v.   force out of an accustomed area

e: Government authorities worry that they lack the means to *uproot* the guerrillas from the Andean region.

Thousands of families have been *uprooted* by flooding in southern provinces.

origin: root—underground base of a plant

usher—v.   inaugurate; introduce; precede
e: Roosevelt's New Deal *ushered* in an era of governmental intervention in the marketplace.
The diplomats were *ushered* into a lounge to wait for the premier's arrival.
origin: usher—attendant who shows people to their seats

vindicate—v.   clear from blame
vindicative—adj. e: The jury fully *vindicated* him of murder charges, but convicted him of possession of an illegal weapon.
The deposed leader says history will *vindicate* her in the end.

vow—n.   formal declaration; solemn promise
vow—v. e: The president has *vowed* to increase funding for the country's poor outlying areas.
She acknowledged defeat in the election, but *vowed* to run again.

wage—v.   engage in, such as a war
e: The board of trade's retail bureau has *waged* a psychological war against shoplifters.
This year's first budget battle has been *waged* with rhetoric.

waive—v.   put aside; give up
waiver—n. e: The Guatemalan government has announced that it will *waive* diplomatic immunity for Dora Caceres.
The defendant has *waived* the right to a lawyer, hoping to attract sympathy from the jury by defending himself.

wake—n.   a track or path left behind; aftermath
e: In the *wake* of the president's declaration, the American people supported the British.
Stocks fell today in the *wake* of the resignation of the Federal Reserve Board chairman.

wares—n.   articles of commerce; goods
e: A slowdown in consumer spending puts a major burden on developing countries that must sell their *wares* to richer nations.
A growing number of street-corner vendors selling their wares is taken as a sign of a growing private economy.

wary—adj.   watchful; attentive; cautious
wariness—n. e: The Soviet leader says he is approaching next week's summit with both hope and *wariness*.
Foreign firms have been *wary* about entering the Chinese market, afraid of any quick policy changes.

weary—adj.   very tired; fatigued
weary—v. e: The set of laws just passed are designed to begin a new, prosperous era for a *weary* bank industry.
The chairman has been *wearied* by years of fighting for control of the board.

weather—v.   withstand a difficulty

    e: Most economists believe that the world economy can *weather* the present instability if world leaders work together.

    Reagan seems to have *weathered* the Iran-Contra affair, but it has cost him a great deal of popularity.

    origin: weather—withstand bad weather

wedge—v.   force into limited space

wedge—n.   e: The Swiss city has been described as 4 million people and 1 million cars *wedged* into a narrow trench between green mountains.

    Tokyo has been tightly *wedged* between the need to trim its huge budget deficit and the continuing push to increase spending.

weed out—v.   eliminate useless elements

    e: Inferior production methods are *weeded out* in this technocratic society.

    The laws were aimed at *weeding* out the undeserving from the welfare programs.

    origin: weed—unwanted plant

weigh—v.   consider the value of; ponder

    e: MX panels are now *weighing* the deployment of up to two hundred new missiles.

    The governor is rumored to be *weighing* the possibility of running for president.

weird—adj.   odd; strange; supernatural

    e: State leaders are debating a law to get rid of several old, *weird* statutes.

    Several residents have reported seeing *weird* objects in the sky; local officials can offer no explanation.

whim—n.   capricious idea; impulse

whimsical—adj.   e: Internal sources say the colonel is crazy, and that his military moves are made simply to satisfy his *whims.*

    She claims she decided to put her money into gold on a *whim*, but it has quickly doubled her net worth.

whine—v.   complain in an annoying way

whine—n.

whiney—adj.   e: In the past the way to stay world-class competitors was not to *whine* and procrastinate, but to boldly seek out new markets.

    This time the president could not dismiss the student protests as "endless liberal *whining*."

wield—v.   exercise; use, as in power

    e: Kissinger still *wields* a considerable amount of power even though he holds no formal office.

    A few corporations *wield* influence over the whole European market.

windfall—n.   unexpected gain or advantage

    e: The Congress enacted a *windfall* profits tax to take advantage of high oil prices.

    The million-dollar lottery win was a *windfall* for the former auto worker.

    origin: windfall—something brought down by the wind

wind up—v.   bring or come to a conclusion
   e: The agreement will *wind up* nearly three years of talks working out the details of the joint-venture agreement.
   The 1982 campaign is *winding up* this weekend, and candidates are making last-minute efforts to win over undecided voters.

wink—v.   twinkle; avoid seeing; to close and open the eyelids quickly
   e: The young lady *winked* to get his attention.

wrangle—v.   dispute noisily; quarrel
wrangle—n.   e: After late-night *wrangling* behind closed doors, the conference came up with a final statement of unity among all the country's major parties.
   The former president's daughter was involved in yet another *wrangle* with police during a protest of the present South African policy.

wreck—v.   destroy; tear down
wreck—n.
wreckage—n.   e: Both sides of the joint venture accused each other of *wrecking* the enterprise.
   The Saudis believed that the proposed prices were too high and threatened to *wreck* the market.

wretched—adj.   deeply afflicted; distressed; inferior
wretchedness—n.   e: The government has promised continued aid to the *wretched* poor of El Salvador.
   The *wretched* quality of the goods turned out by state factories makes them impossible to export.

wry—adj.   twisted (facial features); dryly humorous
   e: "This is a challenge to the authority of all Latin American governments," the general said with a *wry* grin.
   Her *wry* sense of humor has won her a reputation as tough competitor.

zippy—adj.   brisk; snappy
zip—v.
zip—n.   e: Few expect a *zippy* rebound of the economy; though slow, sustained growth is possible.
   After his morning meetings with Gorbachev, Bush *zipped* over to the American embassy for talks with Soviet dissidents.